The Story of Two Guys
Who Wanted to
Own a Restaurant*

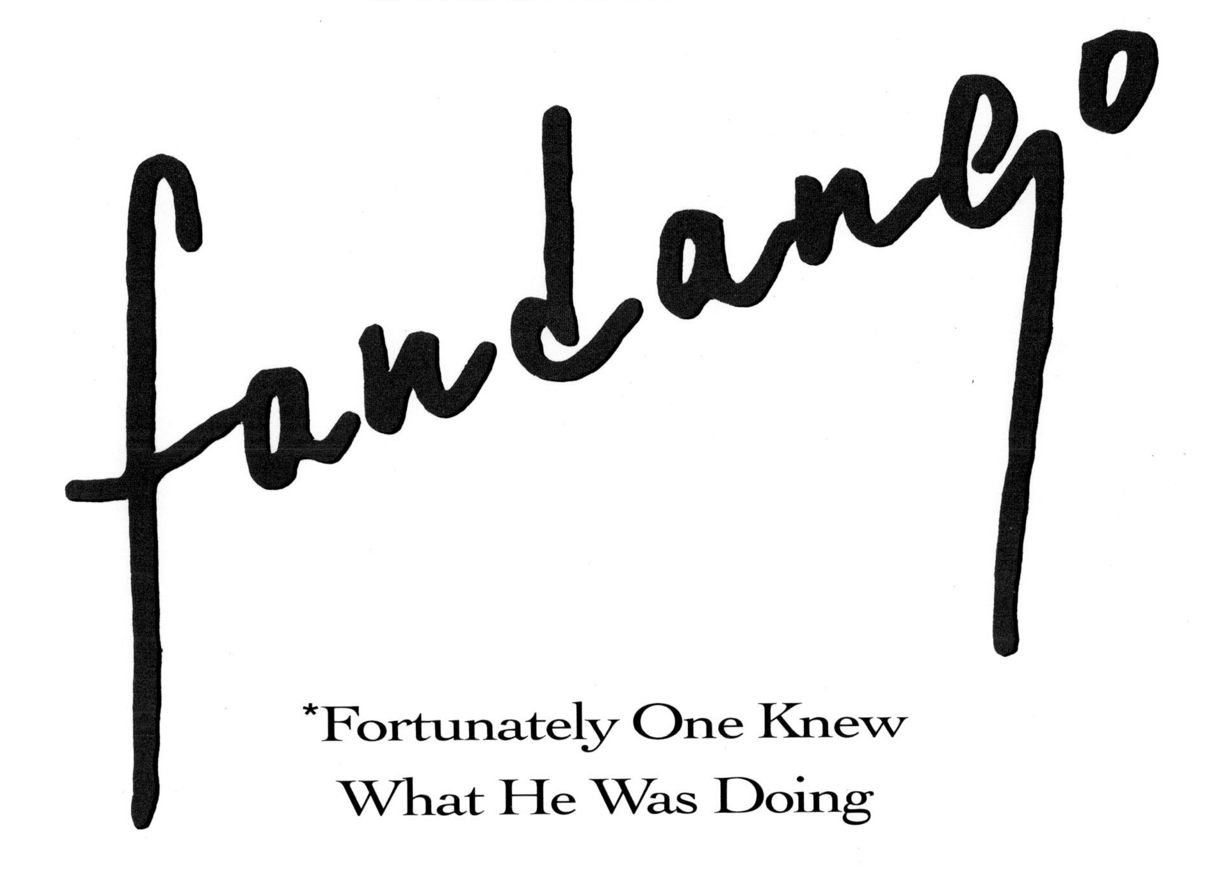

*Fortunately One Knew
What He Was Doing

BY ALAN F. SHUGART

CARMEL, CA

Permission Department
Carmel Bay Publishing Group
Post Office Box 222543
Carmel, CA 93922-2543

Library of Congress Cataloging in Publication Data: No. 93-071413

Fandango: The Story of Two Guys Who Wanted to Own a Restaurant*
*Fortunately One Knew What He Was Doing

By Alan F. Shugart

A true story with recipes.

ISBN: 1-883532-00-0

1) Cookery, Mediterranean, Cuisine of the Sun
2) Fandango (Restaurant: Pacific Grove, CA)
☎ (408) 372-3456

Design by Melissa Thoeny
Photography and food styling by Patrick Tregenza
Principal photography ©1993 by Patrick Tregenza
Food styling, flowers, and props by Julie Levitt

First Printing 1993

First Edition 1993

1 2 3 4 5 6 7 8 9 10

Produced by Mandarin Offset
Printed and bound in Hong Kong

CONTENTS

Introduction	i
Fandango: The Story	1
Fandango Fare: The Recipes	53
Brunch	55
Lunch	61
Entrees	69
Prix-Fixe Dinner	97
Desserts	101
Acknowledgments	107

INTRODUCTION

At a wedding reception one year and one day ago, Al Shugart, my business partner, came to me with an idea. He said he wanted to write a book about Fandango, our restaurant. He asked if I would—from time to time over the next few years—jot down ideas that could be included in the book.

"Sure," I said, although I did not pay too much attention to this idea of his that seemed to come out of the blue. My wife, Marietta, and I were enjoying the party too much to be concerned about a vague project that was so far in the future.

But Al came back to our table an hour or so later, totally charged and energized. "We will get started now," he said.

Marietta and I must have looked confused.

"The book about Fandango," he said. "I have already lined up someone to help us with it."

The looks Marietta and I exchanged were not without dread. This was no longer something in the future. It was to happen now.

That should not have surprised us. We have always known that when Al makes up his mind to do something, there is no stopping him.

Two days later we had our first meeting. I was not sure then—nor really for the next seven or eight months—what the book would finally be about, or even that it would ever be a reality. But here it is, one year and one day later—and here is the book about our restaurant.

As we say in France—*Et voila!*

Pierre

Pierre Bain
9 August 1993

FANDANGO

"Then I commended mirth, for a man hath no better thing under the sun than to eat, and to drink, and to be merry."
—ECCLESIASTES 8:15

The story of Fandango isn't exactly a Horatio Alger story, but it is about success. It's the story of two guys who wanted to own a restaurant—one of whom knew what he was doing.

It's also a story about four partners who came together as much for fun as for profit and—I'm happy to say—achieved both.

I think everybody has a hidden desire to be in the restaurant business. I don't know why. It's really a terrible business to be in. The hours are long and the prospects for success are grim. I've seen figures that put the failure rate for new restaurants around ninety percent.

I slipped into the restaurant business through the side door. Most of my career has been spent in the electronic-computer industry—I've been connected with it since its early days. After graduating from the University of Redlands in Southern California with a degree in engineering/physics, I worked for both IBM and Memorex. Deciding it was more fun to work for myself, I founded Shugart Associates and, later, Seagate Technology. Today, I'm CEO and president of Seagate, which, arguably, is the world leader in the design, manufacture, and sale of computer hard drives. In between all that high-tech stuff I've also taken some time to fish commercially for salmon and to just kick back and loaf.

AS YOU MIGHT GUESS BY THE SEAGATE LOGO ON MY GLASSES, I'M STRONG ON BUSINESS PROMOTION.

Throughout my life—no matter what my "day job" was—the idea of having a restaurant always appealed to me. I'm not a heavy drinker, but I like the social aspect of bars and restaurants. I think if I lived in England I'd be a regular at one of the pubs.

When I lived in Santa Clara in the mid-seventies I used to hang out at a restaurant called Lorenzo's, a gathering spot popular with Santa Clara high-tech people. After I got

to know the owner and the bartender I started thinking more and more about the restaurant business.

A few years later I moved to Santa Cruz and, with a couple of friends, bought The Castaways, an established neighborhood bar. My friends ran it, although I'd fill in behind the bar from time to time.

"Quickly, bring me a beaker of wine so that I may whet my mind and say something clever."

—Aristophanes

Learning about the bar business from the inside was fun—and educational. I realized that part of a bar's atmosphere comes from the patrons and part from the owners. So, since I was one of the owners, I'd sit at the bar and get to know the people.

Most of them came there for the social aspect. We had a few heavy drinkers—people who came in at six in the morning to get a shooter, because it was the first drink of the day they could get. But they were a small minority. Overall, our regular customers came in for the atmosphere and because they liked to socialize with each other. They considered The Castaways a home away from home.

My daughter, Teri, was going to the University of California, Santa Cruz, at the time, and used to pull a Sunday shift behind the bar. She viewed the place the same way I did. For one of her classes, she drew on her observations to write a paper on the social aspects of a neighborhood bar. She used The Castaways as a vehicle, but changed the names of the people to protect the innocent.

It was a good paper, and netted her a "pass" in their "pass/fail" grading system. (I'm sure it was worth an A.) Although it was all her doing, I like to think my contribution may have helped a little bit. I supplied the title: "Home Sweet Budweiser."

My experience with The Castaways whetted my appetite for bigger things, literally and figuratively. There, we served cheese and crackers, and that was about it for food. I decided I was ready to open a real restaurant. I approached an old friend of mine—in fact he'd been a bartender at Lorenzo's—and proposed opening a restaurant in Santa Cruz County.

He liked the idea, so I went ahead and bought a piece of property on Scotts Valley Drive in Scotts Valley, just north of Santa Cruz.

And then I really got into it. I had a restaurant designed, hired a kitchen consultant, had the site graded, got approvals to build it.

It was going to be a fancy restaurant. Probably a little too fancy for rural Scotts Valley. But we hoped to attract people from the other side of the hill—the Silicon Valley and San Jose area.

We were going to call the restaurant Maxim. I even had a designer make me a match book with the Maxim logo on it.

During the time we were considering the restaurant I decided it wouldn't hurt if I knew a little bit about the business. I signed up for a few courses at Cabrillo College, a local two-year college that offered a number of night courses dealing with the restaurant industry.

One of the courses I took was called Restaurant Management. As its name implied, it dealt with the nuts and bolts of running a restaurant. The other course was Meat Analysis. Kind of a pedestrian name, but it was an interesting course. It was "Everything You Ever Wanted to Know About Meat"—and a little bit more. We learned about the different cuts of meat and how to get the best buys. We even took field trips—including one to a slaughterhouse.

I really enjoyed the courses. I actually got A's in both, because I was so interested in them. I should have been that interested back in my undergraduate days at the University of Redlands.

I LEARN THE ROPES IN THE SALMON-FISHING BUSINESS.

Despite all my enthusiasm, the restaurant never got off the ground. We were just starting Seagate Technology, and I didn't have the time to deal with opening a new restaurant. So, I sold the property. It was a little disappointing, but now I'm glad things worked out the way they did. I'm sure I'd have lost my shirt, because neither my partner nor I really knew the restaurant business.

Still, I had some good ideas. In designing the restaurant I placed a lot of importance on its atmosphere.

In the restaurant business, it's a given that you've got to have good food and good

"There is no love sincerer than the love of food."

—GEORGE BERNARD SHAW

service. But that isn't enough. You've also got to have an appealing atmosphere.

Over the years I'd noticed that the bar business was cyclical. Certain bars seemed to come into and go out of favor every three or four years. Bars could survive those fluctuations, riding out the downside of the cycle. But if you were in the restaurant business your margin was too close. You had to avoid the cycles of popularity. And the way you did that was to provide an appealing atmosphere that gave the restaurant consistency.

Unfortunately, atmosphere is something nobody can define. What works at one location doesn't necessarily work at another. If you could define atmosphere—and find a way to package it—you could make a fortune. And you could save a lot of restaurants from going under.

After I sold the Scotts Valley property I put the idea of having a restaurant on the back burner. I had too much to do at Seagate. It was a bit of a letdown, but not a disaster. I actually made a profit on selling the property. Amazing. My first venture into the restaurant business and I came out ahead. That's more than most restaurateurs can say.

Although I was out of the business, it didn't lessen my interest in restaurants as social gathering places.

ON TO PEBBLE BEACH

"For all that moveth doth in Change delight."
—EDMUND SPENSER

In the summer of 1981 my wife, Rita, and I bought a house in Pebble Beach and made the move from Santa Cruz. We didn't completely settle in just then. The house was brand-new, but Rita decided to remodel part of it. She wasn't acting on a whim. She's a terrific cook, and she wanted to redesign the kitchen for serious food preparation.

I thought that was fine—for the long run. But it meant that for several months the bar and the kitchen would be out of commission. It meant that when I came home from Seagate at night I couldn't just sit and have a drink in my own comfortable bar.

But all wasn't lost. Our new home was close to Club XIX, the bar and restaurant at The Lodge at Pebble Beach. As elegant as it was, the Club XIX bar still had a few things in common with my down-to-earth bar, The Castaways: It had atmosphere and it was a social gathering place. And for me, it actually was my neighborhood bar.

Typical of Club XIX's employees, bartender Frank Charland knew his craft. Besides being friendly and outgoing, he was bright and witty. He—as much as the spectacular location—contributed greatly to the atmosphere of the establishment.

The clientele at Club XIX covered a broad spectrum. You might be sitting next to an amateur golfer from the Midwest who'd just realized his dream of playing the Pebble Beach Golf Links, a Hollywood idol escaping the madhouse of Southern California, or the CEO of a Fortune 500 company laying the groundwork for a corporate merger.

"One cannot think well, love well, sleep well, if one hasn't dined well."
—VIRGINIA WOOLF

One evening at the Club XIX bar I got talking with a guy I'd never seen before. It was an easygoing conversation, ranging from sports to space technology. I was impressed by his knowledge and obvious intelligence. We chatted for a half hour or so, then he said he had to meet someone, and left the bar.

After he left it occurred to me that we hadn't introduced ourselves. Out of curiosity, I asked Frank if he knew who the guy was.

"Sure," Frank said. "That was Alan Shepard, the astronaut."

RITA SHUGART

"Energy is Eternal Delight."
—WILLIAM BLAKE

Rita didn't give up on our kitchen until the remodeling made it absolutely impossible to cook there. For several months we were going to have to eat out every night. Many women would welcome that prospect. Not Rita. She enjoys dining at good restaurants, but she also loves to cook. And, as I said, she's a terrific cook. Actually, she's a terrific chef; according to her, I'm a cook.

It's not surprising that she's terrific in the kitchen. Although I may be prejudiced, the fact is, she's terrific at everything she tries.

When we first met she'd just started working for IBM as an entry-level secretary. By the time we married, in 1979, she was putting out a commercial analysis newsletter for them. She had to quit, since my company was one of the businesses she was supposed to analyze.

That didn't slow down her activities any. She established R.K. Shugart, her upscale clothing store in Carmel, which she still manages; founded Briarcliff Academy, a private grammar school that was eventually incorporated into the prestigious Robert Louis Stevenson School; served on the board of the Monterey County SPCA-Humane Society; and brought up three wonderful daughters. She's also raised any number of household pets, as well as the numerous show horses she boards at her daughter Jill's ranch. The horses are to be expected, since her daughter Dana is a champion rider.

RITA SHUGART WITH FRIEND WINSTON (AKA PIGLET)

Oh, and she plays bridge, too. As of spring 1993 she had more than 2,500 master points. Her partner, professional bridge player Bobby Goldman, ranked number three in the nation in total master points earned during 1992. Rita ranked number ninety. Together they finished third in the 1992 Fall National Open Board-a-Match event.

At the same national tournament she was the only woman player among fifty teams who qualified for the finals of the 1992 Reisinger. Movie star and bridge columnist Omar

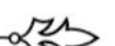

Sharif devoted one of his nationally syndicated columns to a defense strategy Rita used during championship play.

She was also invited to play in a 1992 charity bridge game in Hollywood: Corporate America vs. Hollywood Celebrities. (I forgot to mention that Rita is president of the Monterey Airplane Company, an aircraft-charter company.) I think her team lost, but I don't really remember. (I'm not sure anyone cared.)

In July of 1993 she played in a charity bridge game in Washington, D.C., the third annual Corporate America vs. Congress competition. The Congressional team was made up of three senators, five representatives, and a judge from the National Labor Relations Board. The Corporate America team was captained by Warren Buffett, CEO of Berkshire Hathaway, Inc. Rita, the only woman on the team, replaced the late Malcom Forbes, who'd played in the first two competitions. Not surprisingly, the event was covered by both the *Washington Times* and the *Wall Street Journal.* Although Corporate America trailed late in the going, Rita and her partner, Jimmy Cayne, CEO of Bear Stearns, pulled their team to victory in the final hand.

Along with her willingness to work hard, she also has a sense of fun. When she was on the board of the Monterey County SPCA, she and another board member came up with an idea for an unusual auction. They persuaded a number of prominent local architects to design houses for animals. They then asked local contractors to build them. When the houses were auctioned off, the SPCA made good money and everybody involved had a lot of fun. (And our dogs ended up living in a $10,000 dog house!)

Rita loves to entertain. Every year she puts together a Christmas party for about 150 people. She does all the baking and most of the cooking. It's a blast. It starts about seven in the evening and the last guest doesn't usually depart until about two in the morning.

"A feast is made for laughter, and wine maketh merry."

—Ecclesiastes 10:19

Then there are the special parties. During the 1993 AT&T Pebble Beach National Pro-Am golf tournament, she threw a cocktail party for Bernie Carballo, the Senior Vice President for Sales and Marketing at Seagate. Bernie has been a scratch golfer, and he was making his first appearance in the event. The invitations to the party read: "Please join Rita and Alan Shugart for a cocktail party to get a closer look at Bernie Carballo."

Later Rita planned to shepherd him to the AT&T in her red Ferrari. She'd had

magnetic signs made for the sides that said: "Bernie Carballo—Cuban Celebrity." I thought it would be a stunning way for Bernie to show up at the first tee. He didn't. Still, the look on his face when he saw the signs was worth the cost of having them made.

THE SHUGART MENAGERIE
(*THE ZOO* © WILL BULLAS)

Rita is full of surprises. I'm a hard one to buy gifts for, but she always comes up with something unique to surprise me. One Christmas she gave me an original three-by-six-foot oil painting of all our pets done by Will Bullas, one of my favorite Carmel artists.

On a recent birthday she caught me again. Several months earlier I'd returned from a business trip to the Seagate operation in Thailand. I'd raved about a wonderful statue I'd seen, a life-size, brass cloud leopard on display in the lobby of the Bangkok Hilton Hotel. It really was a striking work of art. I didn't mention it again, but when I came home from work on my birthday, there was its mate, sitting in the middle of our living room. Rita had contacted the management of the Bangkok Hilton and learned that the sculptor had made a pair of the leopards. She'd been able to track down the other leopard and buy it in time for my birthday. It now graces the entry to Seagate headquarters in Scotts Valley.

But back to the remodeling: When the kitchen got so Rita could no longer cook in it, we ate out all the time. Inconvenient, but advantageous. We went to restaurants throughout the Monterey Peninsula region—an area renowned for good dining.

Of the many fine restaurants we visited, Club XIX was our favorite. We soon became regulars there and became friends with manager Pierre Bain and his wife, Marietta.

They were a remarkable couple, filled with energy, intelligence, charm, and dedication to their work. Neither Rita nor I take long to make judgments. We're quick studies, and we liked Pierre and Marietta from the start. Our feelings never changed. That's why—when the time came—we were delighted to become business partners with them.

I was back on the restaurant track. All I needed now was a restaurant.

THE SEARCH

"Seek and ye shall find."
—MATTHEW 7:7

Finding the right restaurant to buy turned out to be a great deal harder than I thought it would be. We combed the Monterey Peninsula, but nothing really caught our eye.

As the axiom goes, the first three things you look for in buying a restaurant are: LOCATION, LOCATION, LOCATION.

Certainly location was an important consideration for us, but location alone wouldn't do it. High on my list of criteria was the old indefinable quality: atmosphere. We didn't know what we were looking for exactly, but we figured once we stumbled across it we'd recognize it.

One of the real problems was comparing any possible site with Club XIX. Besides such intangibles as name recognition and a guaranteed upscale clientele, Club XIX had incredible atmosphere and was located in one of the most beautiful spots on earth. How do you compete with a view that stretches out past the fabled 18th hole of the Pebble Beach Golf Links, across Carmel Bay, and on past the headlands of Point Lobos to the Pacific Ocean and the horizon?

For a while we thought we'd found the right place in Heritage Harbor, the commercial development next to Monterey's Fisherman's Wharf. We were so sure of it, Pierre gave notice to the Pebble Beach Company that he'd be leaving.

The night we decided on that property, Pierre, Marietta, Rita, and I were all having dinner together. I asked Pierre how much it would take to start the process.

He said, "About $200,000."

I turned to Rita and asked, "Have you got a checkbook with you?"

She did. On the spot, I wrote out a check to Pierre for that amount. I had total confidence in him. My philosophy is, either you trust someone or you don't. At Seagate, when we started our operation in Singapore, we gave the guy we hired to run it a check for $50,000 and told him to go open a checking account.

"You'll have no scandal while you dine, but honest talk and wholesome wine."
—ALFRED, LORD TENNYSON

That caught our accountants' attention fast. They said, "What if he just cashes the check and takes off?"

I told them, "Boy, what a cheap lesson that would be!"

And it would have been a real bargain. For only $50,000 we'd find out early on that somebody who'd eventually be handling millions of our dollars was a crook. (He wasn't, I'm happy to say.)

I've always done that. Either you believe in somebody or you don't.

I can't remember when I decided to go into business with Pierre, but I know I liked and trusted him from the start. I also knew he could run a good restaurant.

As it turned out, the deal fell apart at the very last minute. As disheartening as it was at first, eventually we all felt relieved. Talking it over, we discovered that we'd all had some reservations about the place—feelings that we couldn't pinpoint, but which amounted to a sense that the restaurant wasn't a proper fit for the four of us.

However, my offer to Pierre stayed on the table.

I did want a restaurant. And I did want Pierre to run it. I'd seen how much he added to the charm of Club XIX, and I knew that when we had our own restaurant he'd foster the same sort of atmosphere. Our place might not be able to compete with the view from Club XIX, but it would match that restaurant in elegance and in the excellence of its classic French cuisine.

At least that's what I had in mind.

And then Pierre took me to a restaurant in nearby Pacific Grove that specialized in French, Spanish, and Basque provincial cooking, and announced that this was it.

"The discovery of a new dish does more for human happiness than the discovery of a new star."

—Anthelme Brillat-Savarin

Fandango had won his heart.

To tell the truth, it hadn't won mine.

For one thing, it didn't have a sit-down bar. There was a small bar there—a sort of ledge near the service bar—but I couldn't see myself sitting down there and having a drink after work. I couldn't envision a successful restaurant where you couldn't sit right at the bar.

For another thing, it wasn't a classic restaurant like Club XIX or Maxim—the restaurant I'd envisioned years before. Throughout our search, I'd been thinking in

THE PYRENEES CONNECTION

Fandango Restaurant has roots in French, Spanish, and Basque traditions—as does the Monterey Peninsula. In 1786 the first non-Spanish foreigners to visit Spain's colonies in California sailed into Monterey Harbor. The ships were part of a French scientific expedition headed by Jean François Galaup de La Pérouse. La Pérouse kept a journal (part of which can be found in *Monterey in 1786: The Journals of Jean François de La Pérouse,* Introduction and Commentary by Malcolm Margolin, Heyday Books, Berkeley, CA) in which he made particular note of the "Spanish hospitality" shown to himself and his companions. Father Junipero Serra had died two years earlier, and the new president of the California missions was Fermín Lasuén, a Spaniard of Basque descent. La Pérouse singled out Father Lasuén as "one of the most worthy and respectable men I have ever met." He wrote of his first meeting with the missionary: "We were received like the lords of manors when they first take possession of their estates." Although the reception was elegant, the food was pedestrian. One of the showpiece dishes they were served was a vegetable soup called, *pozole* (an Aztec word), which was made from wheat, maize, peas, and beans. It wasn't exactly *haute cuisine*, and La Pérouse didn't say whether he liked it or not. From other comments he made, it would seem that fine manners were more the order of the day in Old Monterey than fine dining. Or fine anything else. La Pérouse noted that the missionaries were "so austere as to their own comforts that they have no fireplace in their chambers, though the winter is sometimes severe." Had La Pérouse stayed at home he could have dined much better—and kept warmer, too—at the Hotel Bain in Comps-sur-Artuby in the south of France, the family restaurant still owned by the family of Fandango's co-owner Pierre Bain. At the time La Pérouse made his expedition to the New World, the Hotel Bain had already been serving travelers for more than half a century.

Father Lasuén hosts La Pérouse at Carmel Mission. (Courtesy, Bancroft Library)

terms of white linen tablecloths and *haute cuisine.*

But Pierre was so adamant that it would work, I went along with him. I didn't want him as a partner just because of his charm and strength of character. The fact was: He knew the business.

As CEO of a company employing some 43,000 people, I have to delegate authority. But I happen to be a delegator anyway. That was my style even when I had only two people working for me.

Rita and I share that philosophy. She applied the principle in raising her daughters, always letting them know that she trusted them and had confidence in them.

Recently I teased her daughter Mia, "You know," I said, "I just can't figure out how you and your sisters turned out so well."

Mia laughed. "If we did," she said, "it's because mom always let us make our own decisions."

"He was an ingenious man that first found out eating and drinking."

—Jonathan Swift

So, Pierre had made his decision, and I felt committed to go along with it. That decided, I started looking on the bright side.

For one thing, I liked the parking lot. A real key to a restaurant's atmosphere is its accessibility. How easy is it to get to? If you have to walk a long way to a bar or restaurant, you're probably not going to go there.

When I realized that the parking lot next to Fandango was full of shoppers during the day and empty at night, I thought, "Wow! Who owns it? We'll have to make some kind of an arrangement with them." (As it turned out, the city owned it and we didn't have to make an arrangement.)

So, we went for it. I didn't have anything specifically against the place—it certainly had warmth and charm—and the parking turned me on. But the deciding factor was Pierre's enthusiasm.

Now I was entering the restaurant business for real, and Pierre—who for twenty years had been the dominant figure at Pebble Beach's Club XIX—was about to embark on a new, uncharted course.

PIERRE BAIN

"The most magical of all the provinces of France is Provence."
—WAVERLY ROOT, FROM THE FOOD OF FRANCE

If there's such a thing as Restaurant DNA, Pierre's genes are packed with it. He was born in Provence at the Hotel Bain in Comps-sur-Artuby, the inn his family has owned and operated since 1737.

That's right—1737!

To put it in perspective: When the Bains first opened for business George Washington was five years old.

Staying in business for more than two and a half centuries should be good enough to put the Bains in the *Guiness Book of Records*. And—as a matter of fact—they're there.

THE HOTEL BAIN,
COMPS-SUR-ARTUBY,
PROVENCE, FRANCE,
FOUNDED IN 1737

Like the Monterey Peninsula, Comps-sur-Artuby is beloved by tourists. It's located at the gateway to what's been called "The Grand Canyon of the Verdon," an area travel writers have compared with Yosemite. In the summer months the hordes of visitors give Comps-sur-Artuby a cosmopolitan air, but when the winter snows seal off the roads to the canyon, it reverts to a small village of about 250 people.

As the firstborn son, Pierre seemed destined to follow in his father's footsteps. He would make his career at the hotel, eventually managing it, carrying on a tradition that had been passed from father to son since the eighteenth century.

As they grew up, Pierre and his three brothers all worked at the hotel during the summer.

During the winter they attended boarding school in Nice, about an hour's drive from Comps-sur-Artuby. After high school—to develop his skills in the business— Pierre

went on to the hotel school in Nice, where he spent three years.

As part of his training, he planned to work one year in an English-speaking country and one year in Germany, German being his third language. After that he'd come back and work at the Hotel Bain, preparing himself for the day when he'd be running it.

PIERRE'S GRANDMOTHER IN THE KITCHEN OF THE GRAND HOTEL BAIN, CHOPPING MEAT AND PREPARING COUSCOUS

That was the plan.

As it happened, the English-speaking country he chose was Bermuda, an environment so desirable he ended up spending six years there.

Finally he decided it was time to return to France. First though, he wanted to get a look at the United States. He applied for and received a green card, which would allow him to make a working tour of the States.

During that tour, he visited San Francisco. He liked the city and decided to work there for a few months before returning to France. He took a job as a waiter at the celebrated French restaurant L' Etoile.

One of the customers he waited on at L' Etoile was Aimé Michaud, then president of Del Monte Properties—which would later become the Pebble Beach Company.

Michaud was so impressed by Pierre that he offered him a job at the new French restaurant he was opening in Pebble Beach.

Pierre wasn't too excited about it. He'd just arrived in San Francisco and wasn't planning to make a move so soon. And—after all—he figured he'd be heading back to France once he'd soaked up enough San Francisco atmosphere.

Still, he decided to give the Monterey Peninsula a look.

That one look did it. He fell in love with the area. Parts of it reminded him of Comps-sur-Artuby. Other parts brought back memories of Bermuda.

And the view from Club XIX itself was as spectacular as anything he'd ever seen.

Besides all the natural beauty, there was a man-made bonus nearby: Laguna Seca Raceway. It was a strong attraction for someone who'd been an automobile-racing buff most of his life.

Pierre quickly decided the Peninsula was for him. He'd come and join the force at Pebble Beach's elegant Club XIX.

PIERRE AND MARIETTA WITH THE REST OF THE BAIN FAMILY IN FRONT OF THE HISTORIC GRAND HOTEL BAIN, 1991

From Scungilli to Escargot

Club XIX opened in 1965 as an Italian restaurant and cocktail lounge. It was a brief incarnation. It closed its doors on May 4, 1966, only to reopen the next day as a French restaurant. On that fine day in May, Pierre began a career that would span the next twenty years.

"At the close of the year, plans were initiated for Club XIX, a new grille and cocktail lounge at terrace level beneath the dining room at The Lodge. The new club room will seat 56 guests. On the same level with the 18th Fairway, it will enable Lodge guests to enjoy the incomparable view of the ocean."

—From Del Monte Properties Annual Report, 1964

There were a few brief interruptions.

In 1967 he left to pursue a career as an airline pilot—he liked fast planes as well as fast cars and had earned a commercial pilot's license during his first year at Pebble Beach. But after months of competing unsuccessfully in a glutted job market with veterans who'd piled up flight time in Vietnam, he decided to return to Club XIX.

He left again in 1969 to return to Comps-sur-Artuby. Ever since he'd headed off for Bermuda, his father had wanted to know when he was coming back. And here it was some seven years later. Pierre decided it was time to return for good.

He left Club XIX in February 1969, just after the Crosby Pro-Am—since supplanted by the AT&T Pebble Beach National Pro-Am—and returned to the family hotel. He worked there until the end of the summer.

It was pleasant for Pierre to return to the scenes of his youth. But as the tourist season wound down, he realized he just wasn't cut out to live in a small village anymore. To paraphrase the old song: "How you goin' to keep 'em down on the farm after they've seen Pebble Beach?"

It was a difficult decision to make, but Pierre and his family took solace in the fact that the Hotel Bain tradition would remain unbroken, since his brother Jean-Marie would take the succession.

Pierre got in touch with the management at The Lodge and said he was coming back to the States. They told him there was an opening for him at Club XIX and asked him to return. He accepted the offer.

Previously he'd started at Club XIX as a waiter and quickly become captain. When he left he was the acting manager. Upon his return from France in the fall of 1969 he assumed the title and duties of full-time manager, a position he would hold until he moved to Fandango at the end of 1986.

During that period, he hosted the great and the near great at Club XIX. Sports stars, political leaders, entertainment figures, Fortune 500 executives, and just plain folks flocked there. Through his experience, drive, and Old-World charm, Pierre made it the place to be on the Central Coast.

PIERRE IN HIS GLORY DAYS AT CLUB XIX

I put a lot of stock in what people's peers think of them—the way they're regarded within their own industry.

Pierre Ajoux knows the restaurant business inside out. He was classically trained at the hotel school in Strasbourg, in the province of Alsace, a school similar to the one in Nice where Pierre Bain studied. The two Pierres have been friends since the mid-1960s, when they met as waiters at Club XIX. Pierre Ajoux still works part-time at Club XIX, and he still has tremendous respect for his colleague.

Says Pierre Ajoux of Pierre Bain: "He is a true great friend of mine. He has a love and knowledge of good food, simple or elaborate—a passion for gastronomy. He is always looking for authenticity and good value. A born restaurateur and innkeeper, he is always in control of the situation. He doesn't get angry or upset, but smiles and overcomes the difficulties at hand—and in the restaurant business, difficulties of all kinds are many. Although he is known and respected by many prominent people, he never falls into the trap of snobbery."

In a few words, Anne Germain, a columnist for the Monterey Herald and author of *Pebble Beach: Then and Now,* caught the spirit of Pierre's reign at Club XIX:

"Club XIX, born and raised at the sensitive and sophisticated hand of Pierre Bain, and nowhere in the world could there be so much to enjoy as there."

The Alexandre Dumas Dinner

"Nothing succeeds like success."
—Alexandre Dumas

Basil (Bill) Coleman presents Pierre Bain with the *Esquire* award.

During the 1969 holiday season Club XIX offered a spectacular "Feast of Noel of Alexandre Dumas." It was based on a menu selected for *Esquire* magazine by Roy Andries de Groot, president of the International Gourmet Society. He'd researched the likes and dislikes of the author of *The Three Musketeers* and found there wasn't much he disliked. (Dumas was great in girth as well as in literary output.)

Dumas also thought big when he made out his guest lists. Sometimes he'd host as many as 500 people—depending on the state of his pocketbook. Besides being hearty, his dinners always featured unusual combinations of foods.

His last book—considered by some to be his greatest—was his *Grand Dictionnaire de Cuisine*. Published in 1873, three years after his death, it's a cookbook as well as a history of and commentary on the art of cooking.

It covers a wide range. He notes in one instance: "Ostrich flesh is not very good. It is tough and tasteless." (He gives no recipe.)

Elsewhere he comments: "There is no doubt that the kangaroo could be most usefully and easily multiplied in Europe, either wild or domesticated. The kangaroo's flesh is excellent, especially when it has grown up in a wild state." (He follows that up with a recipe for Sautéed Kangaroo Filet.)

His entry on donkey begins: "Tastes change."

It's probably best to stop there.

At any rate, the presentation at Club XIX would have done Dumas proud. It was available for several weeks and required at least three days' notice for Chef de Cuisine Marc Vedrine and his assistants, Christian Arnaudin, Jean-Louis Tourel, and Pedro De La Cruz to prepare it.

The first night it was served, Pierre Bain, as maitre d' of Club XIX, began the affair by intoning: "We will start with the champagne," and pouring a Moet et Chandon Dry Imperial, which came from the same house that supplied Dumas.

The soup was a white turtle cream, decorated with red puree of tomatoes and garnished with mussels and oysters in the shell and shrimps. A dry sherry accompanied it.

Next, salmon in an unusual red-wine sauce was served in a bed of flowers. It was garnished with pâté of wild boar, truffles, mushrooms, croutons, and quenelles.

Next, to cleanse the palate, a frothy, fresh-pineapple ice fortified with kirsch was offered.

That was followed by mushrooms and truffles in a cream sauce, served in a pastry shell and backed by a Bollinger's champagne.

Then came the big guns: a pyramid of whole roasted game birds. Pastry cups held pureed peas and beans and currant jelly to be served with the game. A stuffed pheasant in a miniature chef's hat presided over the display.

The salad that followed was said to be taken from Dumas' "secret" recipe. It was followed by six different sherbets served in almond pastry shells, topped by spun-sugar combs. A fine Madeira wine accompanied the dessert. Coffee, cognac, and benedictine closed the three-hour meal.

Basil (Bill) Coleman, then general manager of The Lodge, recently recalled the Dumas Dinner as typical of the style Pierre brought to his work. "When we converted Club XIX to a French Restaurant, Pierre was our guiding light in making it successful. We hoped he'd inject into it the spirit and the essence that we really needed. He did all that, with his personality and his knowledge of food."

Bill knew what he was talking about. An accomplished restaurateur, he started his career as a busboy at the Bohemian Grove, the exclusive retreat in the Sonoma County redwoods. He'd gone to sea at the age of sixteen as a chef aboard a two-masted schooner owned by scientist Templeton Crocker. His voyages took him all over the South Pacific and up and down the coasts of South and Central America. Among the scientists he cooked for were William Beebe, who later became director of the New York Zoological Society's Department of Tropical Research, and Harry L. Shapiro, later chairman of the anthropology department at the American Museum of Natural History.

Before coming to Pebble Beach, Bill spent twenty-five years as right-hand man to the legendary "Trader Vic" Bergeron. He helped run the original Trader Vic's in Oakland and helped set up Trader Vic restaurants in various cities across the country. (He also gave Pierre Trader Vic's recipe for Velouté Bongo Bongo soup, now a favorite at Fandango.)

One of the highlights of Bill's career was hiring Pierre to run Club XIX. "It was the best move we ever made," he says. "Pierre is one of the most outstanding restaurateurs I've ever known—and I've known a lot of them."

As a public relations move, the Dumas Dinner was a huge success, getting good coverage in the local papers, mention in *Esquire* magazine, and great word of mouth.

"But," Pierre remembers, "we lost money on it."

That's not surprising. The tab came to only $30 per person—a steal, even in 1969 dollars.

Marietta Bain

"There is always work, and tools to work withal, for those who will."
—James Russell Lowell

I mentioned that when we were hunting for a restaurant to buy, Fandango didn't impress me right off the bat the way it did Pierre. Marietta felt the same as I did. She and I were both thinking in terms of a fancier place—a classic French restaurant along the lines of Club XIX.

We both loved Club XIX, but from different points of view. My perspective was that of a customer who'd enjoyed a lot of great drinking and dining there.

Marietta saw it from the point of view of someone who'd loved the glamour and excitement of working there for a marvelous restaurateur—who just happened to be her husband. (Marietta, by the way, is one of those rare people who gives work a good name.)

Marietta had met Pierre in 1974, when she was working in a financial advisor's office in Carmel and he was a client. One day while visiting the office he mentioned that there was a weekend job opening up at The Lodge at Pebble Beach.

MARIETTA BAIN

At the time, she had a week-night job in addition to her nine-to-five office job. Bright, dedicated, and a regular dynamo, she always felt you could reach your professional ceiling fast in a small office. To be a success you needed to have your second jobs—and your *third* jobs.

She took Pierre's suggestion and applied for the weekend job at The Lodge. Management liked what they saw, and hired her on the spot. She started as a hostess in February of 1975. A few months later she was offered a weekend afternoon shift to do cocktails outside on Club XIX's patio.

How could a go-getter like Marietta pass up a fourth job?

"The patio had one of the most beautiful views in the world," she says. "I took that job

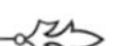

on and there were afternoons when I made more money there than I did all week long at the office."

By May she quit her office job. It wasn't an easy decision. She'd been there six years and had worked her way up to being secretary to the president. It was a risk, stepping away from something as secure as that. But there was a regular shift opening at Club XIX, and she couldn't pass up the opportunity. In her words: "I felt like I was going to work for a dream."

MARIETTA AND PIERRE ON THEIR WEDDING DAY, FEBRUARY 28, 1976, AT CLUB XIX.

She started working a six-day week from May on. Not only did she love the job, there was a mutual attraction between her and her boss. A discreet attraction. She and Pierre didn't go out on an official "date" until October. But then things picked up fast.

By December they were engaged.

By February they were married.

They had a great wedding and reception at Club XIX. And then—happily married—they continued their happy working relationship.

"Pierre has an ability to collect a wonderful crew and work smoothly with it," Marietta says. "He can persuade everyone to do things his way, but with their own style. By the time I came on in 1975, most of the staff at Club XIX had been there ten or twelve years. Whatever other turmoil there was at The Lodge, there was no conflict within the operation of that room."

She was as tireless a worker as Pierre. She took a break in 1977 to have her first child, a son, René. Then—after one week—she returned to work.

Two years later, she left again to have her second child, a daughter, Magali. This time, the ax fell.

The Pebble Beach Company had been acquired by 20th

Ambassador Pierre

Frank Charland, a bartender at Pebble Beach's Club XIX from 1977 to 1982, was always impressed with the unique way Pierre Bain managed the operation. "Club XIX was part of The Lodge at Pebble Beach," he recalls, "but it was definitely Pierre's domain. It was like an embassy within a country, and Pierre was the ambassador. He was a great team player with a genius for getting people to work together. And though he gave people freedom to be who they were, he didn't tolerate unprofessional behavior. That's especially important in a high-profile restaurant or bar. Whoever is in charge has to be sure the people who work for him aren't going to start dropping things and going gaga when celebrities show up. And they certainly showed up at Club XIX.

"I remember a Sunday night when I was just starting there. The bar was deserted, and I was using the time to clean up. When I turned around, I noticed four people had taken seats at the bar: Glen Campbell, Tanya Tucker, George C. Scott, and Jack Lemmon.

Pierre at Fandango with *santons*—saints—hand-crafted dolls that typify the working people of Provence. His "mascot" is in the background.

"Pierre was never intimidated by celebrities. In fact he was oblivious to a lot of movie and TV personalities. Sometimes they'd expect to be known and given special treatment. They'd come in with their arrogant attitudes and Pierre would rise in his own personality and match them—and go above them. No one could ever push him around.

"He had a knack for handling any situation. Maybe it ran in his family. Once, one of his brothers visited from France and took a side trip to Disneyland. He didn't speak English very well and had trouble ordering dinner at his hotel. So he called Pierre at Club XIX and had Pierre order for him. That was a strange situation, the manager of a Pebble Beach restaurant giving an order to a waiter in Anaheim. But when you come to think of it, it was a reasonable approach to the problem.

"Pierre had an appreciation for the unusual. One of his little touches at Club XIX was the big brass cappuccino machine that sat in the middle of the bar. We used it to make Pierre's original cappuccino drink. We served it in a special fluted glass and it was a big hit. No one wanted Irish coffee; they wanted Pierre's Cappuccino Royale.

"That machine was a wonder. It huffed and whined, and puffs of steam shot out the side. It was like the centerpiece of Club XIX."

Note: *Pierre bought the machine from the Pebble Beach Company. It's no longer in operation, but it occupies a place of honor at Fandango, across from the downstairs bar. Pierre refers to it fondly as his "mascot."*

Century Fox. Under their new policy, members of the same family couldn't work together. The policy was sometimes overlooked, but Pierre and Marietta were very much in the public eye. The word came down from above: Marietta must go.

It was devastating for her. "I stayed unemployed for nine months," she remembers. "That's the longest time in my adult life I've been without a job. I don't think I could have ever gone into a more severe depression than I did then. There was no more view of Point Lobos, no more fine china and fine cuisine, no more the excitement and pizazz of dealing with the rich and famous. I was lost. Where else could you find all that on the Monterey Peninsula? The fantasy—which had become my reality—was gone."

But there was an upside. "I think if I'd stayed at Club XIX," she says, "we'd never have left. We wouldn't have been brave or ambitious enough to make the step. After I got out, I wanted Pierre out. I really wanted to see him do something on his own. We always talked about it, but it was so comfortable at Club XIX, we never did it. We'd pursue it right to the edge, and then he'd back off.

"But the longer I was away from there, and the more I saw other operations, the more I realized what an extremely talented man Pierre was. I don't know anyone who's as conscientious and as professional and that really lives the life of a restaurateur as fully as Pierre does."

Marietta took a job at La Boheme restaurant in Carmel, which had been started by the Georis family, who would later found Fandango. She loved being back at work, and she loved the restaurant. "A darling place. Very homey. There was nothing else like it on the Peninsula. It was different enough from what I'd left at Club XIX to make me feel comfortable and make me feel I could pick up and do something new and go in another direction."

She was still working at La Boheme when Fandango was proposed as a possible restaurant for her and Pierre to operate.

Although Pierre loved Fandango from the start, the concept didn't exactly grab Marietta. "Even though I love all the operations the Georis family have created," she says, "I was hesitant. I was still thinking in terms of Club XIX."

She was a Peninsula native who'd grown up in Monterey and had worked in Carmel

"Some people have a foolish way of not minding, or pretending not to mind what they eat. For my part, I mind my belly very studiously, and very carefully; for I look upon it, that he who does not mind his belly will hardly mind anything else."

—Samuel Johnson

and Pebble Beach. Pacific Grove, though, seemed outside that sphere in many ways. Its pace was slower. It was a bit old-fashioned. Maybe even stodgy. Still, she felt Pierre would be successful anywhere.

MARIETTA AND PIERRE WITH THEIR CHILDREN MAGALI AND RENÉ

Besides raising their two children, Marietta had three jobs at the time we bought Fandango: waiting at La Boheme, working for Rita at R.K. Shugart in Carmel, and doing flower arrangements for the Old House in Monterey. She worked at all three jobs right up until we took over Fandango in December 1986.

Since that day she's been full-time at Fandango—which isn't to say she only holds down one job. She's in charge of banquet booking for all parties larger than ten, and she does a little bit of everything else. On a given day she might accept deliveries, bus tables, serve as host or cashier, do all the inside flowers, and be making a menu for a special party.

Whatever she does there, she's an integral part of the operation, adding an essential ingredient to the chemistry that makes Fandango what it is.

She's a gem.

Pedro De La Cruz

"Cookery is become an art, a noble science: cooks are gentlemen."
—Robert Burton

A key element in the new venture was our chef, Pedro De La Cruz. Pierre had worked with Pedro for seventeen years at Club XIX and considered him one of the most talented of the cooks he'd seen during his tenure there.

Marietta, who'd also worked with Pedro at Club XIX, describes him as "one of the most exceptional men I know. A man without an ego. He takes no shortcuts. He has a belief in and dedication to doing the right thing without compromise."

Pedro came to the Monterey Peninsula from his native Philippines while still in his teens. He started as a busboy at Carmel's Pine Inn in 1965 and soon learned his way around a kitchen. In 1967 the Pebble Beach Company hired him as a fourth cook in the main kitchen of the Lodge. After six months he was promoted to third cook. He steadily worked his way up.

He joined Pierre at Club XIX in 1970 as all-around cook and eventually became sous-chef. He continued to learn, studying under various chefs, including some true masters of classic French cooking.

PEDRO DE LA CRUZ

They weren't all the easiest people to get along with. But that, according to Pierre, is a characteristic of most great French chefs.

Pedro, easygoing and tolerant, survived them. What's more, according to Pierre, "He picked up all their good habits and none of their bad ones. He also worked with Swiss, Austrian, and German cooks, selecting what was valuable as he developed his own unique style. Making him chef at Club XIX was the best move we ever made. Among other things, he's a fantastic saucier. He even taught the French cooks at Club XIX some new tricks."

Whenever Pierre contemplated starting his own restaurant, he always had Pedro in

mind as his chef. When we were considering opening a restaurant at the Fisherman's Wharf site, Pedro was uneasy. He'd made a commitment to Pierre, but he thought his friend had made a bad choice.

"I didn't like the location," Pedro recalls. "I figured if they put in the trolley line from downtown Monterey to Cannery Row we'd make a fortune. But if they didn't, we'd go broke. Still, Pierre was my best friend, and if he asked me to leave with him, I couldn't say no."

It turned out they didn't put in the trolley line. But, since we didn't move in, it's a moot point.

A few years later, when we were ready to buy Fandango, Pedro had to face the decision again. Again, Pierre asked him if he'd be willing to leave Club XIX and come with him. Pedro didn't hesitate: "Try me," he said, "I keep my promises."

"Strange to see how a good dinner and feasting reconciles everybody."

—Samuel Pepys

Pierre said, "What happens if we don't make it?"

Pedro laughed. "Then you and I will have to go back on the line."

The truth was, Pedro never doubted Pierre would succeed. Today he says, "I knew everything would work out—and so far we're doing good."

Pierre has just as much faith in his long-time friend and co-worker. How much? He imparted to him the Bain family's centuries-old secret recipe for Couscous Algérois.

Now that's what I call trust.

When we'd been at Fandango a year or so, Ernie Quiddaoen—another cook who'd worked at Club XIX—joined us. By then, Ernie had left Club XIX and gone to work as a chef at one of the major hotels. But he was willing to come to Fandango and work with Pedro and Pierre. He's our sous-chef now and he's a great addition to the Fandango team.

Pierre attributes much of Fandango's success to Pedro. Not just because he's such a master in the kitchen, but also because he's such a positive force in the organization. "When Pedro came with me," Pierre says, "it gave me confidence. As new as we were to owning a restaurant, I at least had a menu, a clientele, and a superb chef who'd been with me for twenty years."

Odds & Ends

YEARLY SERVINGS OF FOOD

MEALS:

Sunday brunches: 7,800

Lunches: 36,500

Dinners: 54,750

FOOD BY MEAL:

Racks of lamb: 10,000

Paellas: 12,000

Swordfish: 6,000

Scallops: 4,000

Bowls of onion soup: 4,000

FOOD BY WEIGHT:

Salmon: 2,000 pounds

Pasta: 4,000 pounds

DESSERTS:

Ice cream desserts: 16,000

Other desserts: 10,000

YEARLY SERVINGS OF BEVERAGES

Beverages (non-alcoholic) 80,000

Espresso and cappuccino: 20,000

Glasses of wine: 30,000

Bottles of wine: 26,000

Imported: 3,000

Domestic: 23,000

MISCELLANEOUS:

Wine labels on hand in 1986: 40

Wine labels on hand in 1993: 450

Least expensive wine: $12

Most expensive wine: $1,550

Indoor tables: 50

Outdoor tables: 6

Kitchens: 2

Mesquite grills: 2

Monthly cost of kalamata olives: $1,000

Average number of requests for charitable donations: 3 per day

A European Concept

"The destiny of countries depends on the way they feed themselves."
—Anthelme Brillat-Savarin

When we bought Fandango at the end of 1986, it was already a going concern. It had been started in 1983 by the Georis family, who'd earned a solid reputation in the area for their two Carmel restaurants, La Boheme and Casanova.

Although there are a dozen good restaurants in Pacific Grove today, when the Georises started Fandango there were far fewer. But they saw the potential there, and decided it would be a good place for them to expand a bit.

Before it was converted to a restaurant, Fandango—just as Casanova had been—was a residence located in a commercial zone. The Fandango conversion began in 1982 and was finished in 1983.

The idea of making it a French Basque restaurant appealed to Walter Georis. At the time he was manufacturing fabric in the Basque country in the Pyrenees Mountains between France and Spain. He decided to include Spanish elements with the French and Basque elements, since the independent-minded Basques feel they don't belong to either France or Spain and travel freely across the Pyrenees.

"Americans are just beginning to regard food the way the French always have. Dinner is not what you do in the evening before something else. Dinner is the evening."
—Art Buchwald

Walter describes the fare he finally arrived at as "rustic food. Lots of beans and pork and lamb and cassoulet-type things."

The term "Renaissance Man" is much abused. It's often applied to anyone who can walk and chew gum at the same time. But when it's used to describe Walter Georis, it has significance.

Besides being a successful restaurateur, he's a painter, a photographer, a furniture designer, and a craftsman. He also composes music. While still in high school he wrote the score for Bruce Brown's pioneering surfing film *Endless Summer.*

Add to that, he's an accomplished winemaker. In fact, wines from his Georis Winery in Carmel Valley are now on the wine list at Fandango. (Could it be more than coincidental that Walter was actually born in a wine cellar in Belgium?)

In naming his new restaurant, Walter drew on his artistic background. "We chose the name Fandango because it's easy to remember. And the Fandango is a lively dance, a little bit rambunctious. The name itself is musical, and it looks good when you write it out."

He spared no pains in decorating Fandango. He visited a factory in France and had them make the chairs to his specifications. He personally made all the tables. To insure the interior stucco walls were authentic in coloring and patina, he did all the plaster work himself.

Walter's attention to detail in the design and operation of the restaurant paid off. Fandango soon became popular because of all the qualities Pierre later saw in it: good food, good fun, good service, and good ambience.

Finally, in 1986, Walter decided to sell the restaurant so that he could devote more time to other projects, primarily the winery he'd built in Carmel Valley.

Because Fandango had been a labor of love for him, he was delighted to pass it on to Pierre Bain. "We came from similar backgrounds in Europe," Walter says. "That's really the secret of Fandango's success. You could look at a complicated approach, but it's relatively simple: one European taking a concept that felt comfortable to him, and the other one picking it up because he could relate to the same things. So, it was natural for Pierre to step into that position and take it one step further by adding his expertise.

"It's almost as though a family member had taken over. When I go there for lunch or dinner or just to visit, I still feel very much at home, which I really appreciate."

Walter's touch didn't end when he sold the restaurant. Several years later, when we built the upstairs addition, we asked him to design the interior for us. He did, and he kept the continuity and the feeling of the restaurant.

"Fill ev'ry glass,
for wine inspires us,
And fires us with
courage, love and joy."

—John Gay

René Cruz

"The cooking of Languedoc is peasant cooking...solid, like the strong Romanesque architecture of the south...its raw materials are substantial and they are put together with gusto."

—Waverly Root, from <u>The Food of France</u>

We're very lucky to have René Cruz as our maitre d'. René is actually an old hand at Fandango, having started work here in 1984, when the Georis family owned the restaurant. Among the customers he greeted back then was Pierre Bain.

"Pierre always loved this place," René recalls. "Among other reasons, it was very European. It had great potential right from the beginning, and I think it was just made for Pierre."

Like Pierre, René hails from the south of France and has spent most of his life in the restaurant business—although he admits Pierre got into the game earlier in life than he. According to René: "Pierre was crawling around a kitchen when he was a baby."

Still, René leaped into the fray soon enough. Born in the Languedoc city of Béziers, by the age of fourteen he was holding down a full-time summer job at a restaurant on the Mediterranean coast between Marseilles and the Spanish border. There, he worked his way up from dishwasher to cook.

RENÉ CRUZ

Before coming to California, René worked at Le Chalet, a popular French restaurant in Arlington, Virginia, that catered to an international clientele from Washington, D.C. He worked as a waiter during the day and as sous-chef at night.

As does Pierre, René clings to his roots in southern France. And whenever he returns there he always tries to stop by Comps-sur-Artuby for a visit to Pierre's family at the Hotel Bain. "By now," he says, "I feel like a member of the Bain family."

In the Fandango family, Pedro, René, and Pierre are a team of three. They're individuals, and they have different opinions, but they don't have big arguments.

One of the great things about Fandango is that we don't have conflicts between the kitchen and the dining room. That's a problem in many restaurants. If a cook and a waiter, or the chef and the maitre d', are fighting, the loser is always the customer.

Like Pierre, René loves automobile racing. He takes only two Sundays off a year: one for the Super Bowl, the other for the grand-prix races at Laguna Seca.

FANDANGO'S ATMOSPHERE IS RUSTIC, CASUAL, COMFORTABLE.

This isn't a recent development. Years ago he took a job for ten days in a Monte Carlo cafe restaurant—just so he could be on hand for the French Grand Prix.

He's been going to Laguna Seca ever since he moved to the Monterey Peninsula. He knows many of the drivers, and when he talks with them he promotes Fandango. And effectively. Bobby Rahal—who won the Indy 500 in 1986—regularly stops by when he's in town. In fact, after winning the CART championship at Laguna Seca in 1992, Bobby held his victory celebration at Fandango. (The week before that he celebrated his wife's birthday there.)

Racing great Mario Andretti is also a frequent visitor.

They say you only get one chance to make a good first impression. That's one reason we're happy to have René representing us at Fandango's front door.

As René says, "Pierre likes to see people leave the restaurant happy so that they'll come back again. I try to start that process as soon as they arrive."

RENÉ CRUZ ON FANDANGO'S ATMOSPHERE

Going to a restaurant is more than just going to a store and buying a steak. You go for the whole experience. If someone goes to a cocktail party, comes here for dinner, and then goes to a club, a film, or a play, we are an important part of their evening's entertainment.

This place is fun. If people come here and they drop a knife on the floor, nobody's going to turn around and look at them. We're not that kind of place. I've come to know most of the people who come here. All the locals. We have stories to share. When we greet our customers, we don't just say, "Hi." We make contact.

Farewell to Club XIX

"A hard beginning maketh a good ending."
—John Heywood

Pierre left Club XIX in November 1986 and embarked on a long-overdue trip. There was pressing business at home, but he realized it might be years before he'd get another chance to visit his relatives in Comps-sur-Artuby.

During the flight to France, he sketched out a plan and a budget for the new restaurant on a yellow legal pad. Gas, electricity, food, wine, employees, the menu, advertising—and a hundred other factors. Since he didn't know what the variables would be, it was a shot in the dark. But he had to start somewhere.

"Wine is sure proof that God loves us and wants us to be happy."
—Benjamin Franklin

Marietta was busy on the home front. She and Pierre had just bought a house in Monterey. Because he was in France, she had to oversee the move by herself, adding a little more spin to her normal whirlwind of activity.

When Pierre returned from France he was eager to get started in the new business. However, he couldn't take physical control of the restaurant until escrow closed on December 30—the next-to-last day of the year.

Earlier our accountants had said there'd be advantages to opening in 1986, if only for a day.

Well, that's all that was left.

We still hadn't reached an agreement on the wine inventory. That day we got the key, we reached an agreement that the Georises would keep the wine. Everything else in the restaurant would be ours.

All the equipment, that is—but no food. There wasn't even a bag of salt there. Still, we decided to open for lunch the next day so that we'd have the restaurant in operation in 1986. It would take a frantic effort, but it could be done.

Pierre and René headed for town with a lengthy shopping list. Late in the afternoon they returned with meat, fish, vegetables, dairy products—all the perishables they'd need for the next day. They popped them into the walk-in refrigerator, breathed a sigh

of relief, then turned to other pressing matters that threatened to overwhelm them.

When Pedro came in the next morning he was greeted with an unwelcome surprise. Everything in the walk-in was frozen. The refrigerator had been left running—but empty—for several weeks. In its eagerness to suck the heat out of anything that came near it, it had solidified our plans in a way we hadn't expected.

So, before we could open up, Pierre and René had to rush out and buy all new produce.

Marietta took solace in the fact that the coffee—at least—hadn't been in the refrigerator. But when she went to start a batch, she realized she didn't know how the machine worked. She learned fast.

Meanwhile, word of our opening had spread and reservations were pouring in. A lot more than we'd anticipated. Thank God for René! His experience as Fandango's maitre d' under the Georises was invaluable. We counted on him to get the flow going, and he pulled us through.

That day, Pedro presided over a kitchen staffed by people he barely knew. Both Pierre and René greeted customers at the door and waited on tables. Marietta tended the cash register, handled the phones, and took part in general trouble shooting, of which there was plenty.

Marietta remembers the day well: "I think it was the very worst day of working I've ever experienced in my life."

Coming from an admitted workaholic, that's pretty strong stuff.

It wasn't just the pace that got to them. Pierre and Marietta were used to working under pressure. The worst thing was the jittery feeling that came with having total responsibility for the operation. At Club XIX the ultimate responsibility for the restaurant fell on the Pebble Beach Company. "But," Marietta recalls, "suddenly everything that could go wrong in a situation was our responsibility. I'd never had that feeling. I could always blame it on somebody else. It could always be the owner, or the chef, or whoever. Now it all fell on us, and it was overwhelming.

"We managed to make it through the day. Finally we cleaned everything up and closed for the night, and that was our New Year's Eve celebration. Some party!"

"Happiness:
a good bank account,
a good cook, and
a good digestion."

—Jean Jacques Rousseau

Small Change

"If it ain't broke, don't fix it."
—American Folk Saying

We never had any thought of changing the name. The fandango, the lively folk dance of Moorish origin, has been popular on the Iberian Peninsula and in southern France since the eighteenth century. Its history parallels that of the Hotel Bain. It's a lively dance, distinguished by exuberance and passion, rather than classical niceties.

That certainly fit with the sort of restaurant Pierre had in mind.

"Fandango, because of Pierre's love for it the first time he saw it, forced him to be who he was. Otherwise, Pierre would have taken another path. The restaurant itself helped form Pierre."

—Marietta Bain

Once we'd met our goal of opening in 1986, we closed down for several weeks to regroup. That gave us a chance to consider changes. But what to change? Pierre and Marietta were tempted to do something to make it more sophisticated.

The cloth lamp shades, for instance, bothered Marietta at first. They seemed so frilly, so old-fashioned. She felt, "We can't live with that. People will laugh at us."

But then she realized she was thinking in terms of Club XIX. Fandango was Fandango—nothing more, nothing less. She and Pierre liked the total feel of the place, and if they picked away at it, that feeling would be gone.

So they stayed with the lamp shades—as unsophisticated as they seemed in comparison to the elegant decor of Club XIX. And they grew to love them. In fact, when they later called on Walter Georis to design the upstairs, he used the same cloth shades. By then everyone accepted the fact that they were exactly right for the place.

We didn't make any major changes in the design of Fandango. We did some repainting, added some things, but didn't take anything away.

The most significant change for us was getting a liquor license. Fandango had been serving beer and wine, but we wanted to provide our customers with a full range of beverages.

That created a stir.

How Dry We Almost Were

"The town [of Pacific Grove] is indeed, a bit of Puritan New England transplanted to the land of the Spanish cavalier."

—Tirey L. Ford, Dawn and the Dons (1926)

Dubbed "The Last Hometown" by its residents, Pacific Grove was the last dry town in California. From the city's founding in 1875 until 1969 you couldn't even buy a beer at a Pacific Grove market.

By the mid-1980s the city had overturned most of its blue laws. There were a couple of liquor stores in town, you could get beer and wine at the grocery stores, and three restaurants operated full bars.

But even though we were technically allowed to have a liquor license for Fandango, a number of the city's residents were opposed to our getting one. They were afraid we'd be bringing a barroom atmosphere to the downtown area.

We had to state our case at a number of hearings—some of them fairly heated. At one of them, a person opposed to our license offered a bewildering rationale for his opposition. As far as we could figure, he was making an ad hominem case against Pierre: He said he'd once dined at Club XIX during Pierre's tenure there, and he thought the onion soup was lousy. That stung.

PACIFIC GROVE, FOUNDED AS A RELIGIOUS RETREAT BY THE SEA, WAS BONE DRY FOR 94 YEARS.
(THE PAT HATHAWAY COLLECTION)

Fortunately, the city council overlooked the slur on Pierre's character. And after we'd had our final say, most of the opposition to us melted away. In fact, a man who'd led that opposition became one of our most fervent supporters.

Mayor Morrie Fisher had supported us from the start, and the council finally cleared the way for our license—with restrictions. It took another three years for us to get the restrictions removed so that we could operate like the other licensed restaurants in town. By that time it was clear that we weren't going to disrupt the pattern of life in Pacific Grove. We weren't fly-by-nighters, seeking a fast profit. We were here for the long run.

In the words of the councilwoman who moved to lift all restrictions: "Fandango is an excellent addition to the community...its track record is impeccable."

Reopening

"By working faithfully eight hours a day, you may eventually get to be a boss and work twelve hours a day."

—Robert Frost

We opened again in late January '87—Super Bowl Sunday, to be exact. It was a hellish day for the Denver Broncos. The New York Giants stomped them 39-20.

It was just as hellish for us. We should have never done anything like that. We thought it would be a way to ease the door open. We didn't think we'd draw much of a crowd, since everybody would be home in front of the TV watching the big game.

JOHNNY MILLER TOOK TOP HONORS AT THE 1987 AT&T PEBBLE BEACH NATIONAL PRO-AM.
(PHOTO BY R.J. GRUBER)

We were wrong. The place was jammed. It was more of a madhouse than our first opening day.

One of the biggest problems was that the Fandango crew wasn't yet a team. Pierre and Marietta had worked with Pedro for years—and they knew René well—but everyone else was new to them. They'd never been in a situation like that before.

But they made it through the day. And the next day. And the day after that.

Soon it was time for the AT&T tournament, and again we were almost overwhelmed—this time for a solid week.

The AT&T crowds were only part of the influx. Because of the reputation Pierre had earned at Club XIX, people were flocking to Fandango to see what he was doing with it. And of course, they were bringing high expectations, which we weren't sure we could meet.

Not long after we opened, the Pebble Beach Company began a remodeling project, which closed Club XIX for about two months.

That was a real bonus for us, although it created a problem. We were actually getting too many reservations.

In the beginning there'd be an hour or hour-and-a-half wait for some of those familiar customers from Club XIX. It was just out of whack, and only time could fix it. It put us in a frenzy, but overall the closing of Club XIX was a godsend for us. It gave people who would normally go there a new place to try.

After three or four months, things began to fall into place. Still, it took another year or so to really get it together.

At Club XIX Pierre had been working with some members of his staff for fifteen years or more. Now it was like starting a new family. Pedro, of course, came with him from Club XIX, and a number of others followed. But it took a while for the new Fandango team to coalesce.

Eventually, those who weren't happy left; those who didn't work out were let go; and the newer members were brought into the fold.

Finally, we were a functional, comfortable family that could work together and enjoy it.

That isn't to say the hard work was over.

The first couple of years were killers. Sometimes Pierre and René would do the door, and the bar, and the cash register, and wait on tables.

The two virtually lived in the restaurant. They'd each work between five and six double shifts every week. They had a cot upstairs so they could catch a nap between shifts. But the telephone was there for reservations, so uninterrupted slumber was a rare event indeed.

Despite the harried pace and long hours, those were exciting times for everyone involved. René says in retrospect, "Those are all good memories. Pierre and I were working every day, not taking vacations, trying to do something better each day. It was hard work, but it paid off."

PIERRE ON
PAYING YOUR DUES

The backbone of a restaurant is the kitchen. That is where you start learning the business. I was in the kitchen at an early age. In those days it was more difficult. Now you buy trout and they are already cleaned. Then, people brought you the trout and you had to clean them, empty them. We served a lot of game. Hares, you had to skin. Chickens and pigeons, you had to pluck. It was a lot of work. Enough to turn anyone away from wanting to cook. But you kept going because you knew pretty soon you would move on and someone else would have to do that work and that someday you would be giving the orders.

CONSISTENCY

"Stability is not immobility."
—PRINCE METTERNICH

The hardest part is behind us. We know that our customers like our menu, the quality of our food, our service, and our atmosphere. Now it's a matter of maintaining our standards and being consistent.

We make changes the way porcupines make love—carefully. It's a delicate business, because some of our customers don't want any change.

They delivered that message a few years ago during the "Great Rack of Lamb Fiasco."

From the beginning, Rack of Lamb Provençal has been one of our specialties. But one night—for reasons I can't even recall now—we took it off the menu.

Bad move. People were furious.

One regular customer vowed he'd never eat at Fandango again unless we restored it.

We assured him we'd be serving it again the next night.

We did. And he came back.

It's been on the menu ever since.

We didn't dare risk a kalamatas fiasco. Kalamatas are the special Greek olives we've been setting out for our dinner guests ever since we opened. They're delicious—plump, salty, satiny, juicy. We use a lot of them, and buy them by the twenty-eight-pound pail. A few years back we paid $36 a pail for them. They were more expensive than ordinary olives, but we thought they were worth it. Then a big freeze blanketed Greece and devastated the crop. The price soared to around $90 a pail.

LIFE IS JUST A BOWL OF OLIVES.

We continued to buy them at that price, figuring it would go down after the next crop. But it stayed up.

What could we do? Our customers love those olives. We love our customers. So, we

stayed with the kalamatas, which now cost us about $1,000 a month. We still think they're worth it.

The changes that we do make are part of our policy of "continuous improvement."

For instance, we changed the way we slice the Rack of Lamb. We used to slice it the same way they do everywhere else. But then René suggested to Pierre that we slice the bone on one side and leave the whole filet together. Pierre liked the idea, so that's how we serve it now.

A STIRRING MOMENT IN THE LIFE OF PEDRO DE LA CRUZ.

And we do add to the menu now and then. Recently we introduced a delicious, tomato-based, fish soup that Pedro created for our Friday soup of the day.

Pierre worried there'd be a rebellion from the New England clam chowder advocates. But no. To Pierre and Pedro's delight, the compliments poured in.

PIERRE ON FANDANGO'S CUISINE

In the South of France, when I was young, we cooked with olives, tomatoes, fish—things that were indigenous.

Later I went away from that kind of food and learned a different type of cooking. I learned in fancy restaurants to prepare much richer food, using a lot of milk and cream. But now, everyone is getting away from such rich foods. They are turning to the kind of food I was raised with. Now, at Fandango, we serve the kind of food we liked in southern France. Those dishes are my roots; They are the cuisine of my mother and my grandmother. I have completed the cycle.

Upstairs at Fandango

"The best way to have two restaurants is to build one on top of the other."
—Pierre Bain

We made one major physical change at Fandango: the addition of the upstairs room. We wanted it to be new and different, but we also wanted it to merge with the downstairs. To insure continuity, we asked Walter Georis to help us design the interior.

We're delighted with the results. Mike McNally, the architect on the project, did a terrific job. Not just on the building itself, but on solving the problems you run into when you have to deal with building codes, water allocations, zoning regulations, and the numerous meetings with such groups as the city council, the planning department, and the architectural review board.

Mike has practiced in Pacific Grove for more than twenty years and has a real feeling for the city—a sense of what's appropriate for "The Last Hometown." Fortunately, by the time we added the second story, Fandango had established a good reputation in the community. Still, Mike held our hand all through the process. The conceptual drawing that we submitted to the city—Mike's color sketch—now hangs on the wall near the downstairs bar. Not only did he give us a good starting point for building the second floor, he gave us an attractive work of art.

MIKE MCNALLY'S CONCEPT OF FANDANGO'S UPSTAIRS ADDITION.

The actual layout evolved during the construction. According to Mike, Pierre changed his mind about nine times on the kitchen—but they weren't whimsical changes. He wanted it absolutely right, so it would function just the way he and Pedro wanted it to. We've got a complete kitchen upstairs, as well as another bar and another mesquite grill. It's really like having a second, independent restaurant.

UPSTAIRS AT FANDANGO AT NIGHT.

Work on the addition went so smoothly that it never interfered with the operation of the restaurant. Thanks to the contractor, Ken Rudisill, head of Harvest Construction in Seaside, we stayed open the whole time.

During the construction, Mike worked closely with Ken. It wasn't hard for Mike to keep an eye on the job—his office looks out on Fandango and he could talk with the work-crew superintendent by two-way radio.

Mike's location provided another bonus for us—and it's ongoing. Since his office is so near to Fandango, he's one of our regular customers.

PIERRE ON EXPANSION

Very quickly our restaurant began to do well. We thought of opening another one, but we decided not to. There are some restaurants where you do not have to be present. You can open a chain of them. But this kind of restaurant needs a lot of personal attention. People expect to see you in person as part of it. When we did expand, we duplicated our ground-floor restaurant on the second floor. It has also been successful. I am convinced: The best way to own two restaurants is to have one on top of the other.

TAKING CARE OF BUSINESS

"Business without profit is not business any more than a pickle is a candy."
—CHARLES F. ABBOTT

In business, you're always looking for an unfair advantage. One that we had in our early days was the fact that Pierre and I knew a lot of people. Those contacts still help us. The AT&T Pebble Beach Pro-Am people buy the whole second floor for the week of the tournament because of Pierre's contacts.

"Wine is the most healthful and hygienic of beverages."
—LOUIS PASTEUR

Those kinds of contacts can help you to get started—but they can't keep you going. The AT&T wouldn't keep coming back if we didn't have good food, good service, and good atmosphere.

And to stay in business, you've got to "take care of business."

In the restaurant-management course I took, the emphasis was on accounting—how you know if you're making or not making money.

You've got to look at your monthly financials really carefully. You've got to keep track and know exactly what percentage of profit you're making on each segment of the business. Problems in one segment of your business can wipe out all the profits from the other segments very quickly.

Pierre has a sharp business sense, and was smart enough to get outside accounting help from the start. Our accountants report to us in excruciating detail. We get a monthly printout that gives the status of 1,150 items of expenditure.

Using that, we can spot trends. For instance, the liquor-gross margin might be going down or going up. If you don't know why it's changing, you'd better find out fast. And then you'd better take action.

Pierre keeps an eye on the whole operation. He and Pedro watch the buying closely, checking the prices and making sure we get the quality of food we want. He and René keep a similar watch on the dining room.

Keeping on top of financial matters is *so* important in a restaurant. You've got to be lean, but you can't be too lean.

PIERRE BAIN AND HIS STAFF GATHER FOR A "CLASS" PICTURE.

PIERRE
ON STAFFING

Good help is hard to find. Once you find good people you want to keep them all year-round. That is one of the reasons we can be consistent, which you have to be to succeed in the restaurant business. You try to run a place as lean as you can— it is part of the business. But if you run lean, you had better be sure everybody shows up. If they do not, you will feel it. And eventually, the customer will feel it too.

You can sometimes squeak by with a limited staff—but not for long. It usually means people have to work double shifts. That's costly, and the people tend to get burned out. It's a temporary measure at best.

Obviously, René can't be on duty all the time, but Denise Marseguerra has proven to be a capable backup person.

Denise came on as a waitress a month after we opened. She had a strong background in the restaurant business and soon demonstrated her intelligence and tenacity.

A few years ago we made her maitre d' downstairs on weekdays and upstairs on

weekends. Because of her personality, talent, and willingness to work hard, she was a very good waitress. Those same qualities now make her a very good maitre d'.

A familiar face—and voice—at Fandango, she always seems cheerful, whether greeting customers at the door, presiding over a banquet, or taking reservations over the phone.

She qualifies that: "Not always cheerful. I think sometimes my kitchen attitude with the staff is different from the attitude I have with our customers. But it has to be. You have to have a firm hand to make things work smoothly."

She does make things work smoothly. And best of all—no matter how hard it gets at times—she makes it look easy.

We have a dozen or so people waiting on tables, and there's a low turnover in that department.

DENISE MARSEGUERRA

The two "deans" of the waiting staff are Peter Borowiak and Wesley Cain.

Peter joined us early in 1987—before our second "grand opening." Born into a family of German restaurateurs, he apprenticed for three years at Hamburg's award-winning hotel *Der Vierjahreszeiten*, learning the business from top to bottom. Subsequently he worked at some of the finest restaurants in the world, including Ernie's and La Bourgogne in San Francisco, where he waited tables. He later worked as a captain at Michel's at the Colony Surf in Hawaii. Even later, he owned and operated restaurants in San Francisco and Mexico City.

"From wine what sudden friendship springs."
—JOHN GAY

Wesley started working for Pierre as a busboy at Club XIX in 1967, while still in high school. After being drafted and serving a tour in Vietnam he returned to Club XIX, where Pierre trained him as a waiter. Later he worked there as assistant manager, learning the ins and outs of the business from Pierre. Not long after Pierre left Club XIX to open Fandango, Wesley joined him.

Peter and Wesley are consummate professionals, with their own following of patrons who ask for them by name. Although they're both steeped in the classic tradition of *haute-cuisine* restaurants, they bring the human touch to their work. They both believe in superb service—with a smile. They contribute a lot to Fandango's ambience.

Don't Spare the Courses

"Penny wise and pound foolish."
—William Camden

The one area where you can never skimp is in the food department. Even if the accountants suggested we cut corners there, Pierre and Pedro wouldn't hear of it. If it came to that, they'd defend the kitchen with cleavers.

Their concern shows. I think the food at Fandango is terrific. Most of the restaurant reviewers who've been here agree. Still, we don't cherish their opinions as much as we do the opinions of our regular customers. So far, they've been leaving the restaurant happy and coming back for more.

I check the financials every month, but I take a hands-off approach to the actual running of the restaurant. I'd never want to tell anybody who's knowledgeable about the restaurant business what they should do—and Pierre knows a hell of a lot more about it than I do.

However—and Pierre will vouch for this—I'm never short of opinions. For instance, as much as I like his Caesar Salad dressing, I think my wife's is even better.

As he says, it's my privilege to prefer Rita's recipe—but that doesn't mean it's going on the menu!

I'm a good customer—a paying customer. I eat at Fandango about twice a week, when I'm not traveling somewhere on business. I pay full price, too, just like any other customer. I realize the restaurant is a business, not a plaything.

I even feel guilty about calling and getting a last-minute reservation when the restaurant's crowded. Once, I called late without giving my name. Because they had a big party booked that night they had to turn me down.

Rita was in the hospital at the time, recovering from back surgery. When I stopped

ONE OF FANDANGO'S PAELLAS IN ITS EARLY STAGES.

by to see her, I mentioned that I'd just tried to get a reservation at Fandango, but that they were full.

She picked up the bedside phone and called the restaurant. Neither Pierre nor René was there, but she told the man who took the call, "This is Rita Shugart. My husband says he wants to have dinner there but he can't get a reservation."

The man said, "No problem, Mrs. Shugart. I'll have a table for him."

And he did.

When I'd called, I didn't have the guts to say, "This is Al Shugart, the co-owner, and I want a reservation." But Rita got me one just like that.

I mentioned that to a friend and he commented, "Al, in the computer world you're known as a captain of industry. On the Monterey Peninsula they know you as Rita Shugart's husband."

PIERRE ON SIMPLICITY

The table at Fandango warms the heart and gives strength and happiness. Our cuisine is simple, traditional, close to the product—without any mystery. What you see is what you get.

By the way, despite my suggestion, Pierre isn't about to replace his Caesar Salad dressing with my wife's. He says, "My Caesar Salad dressing is so popular I wouldn't dare change it. But she has always claimed—God bless her—that hers is better."

Since I don't try to tell Pierre how to run the restaurant I won't press the point. But I do love Rita's recipe. Here it is:

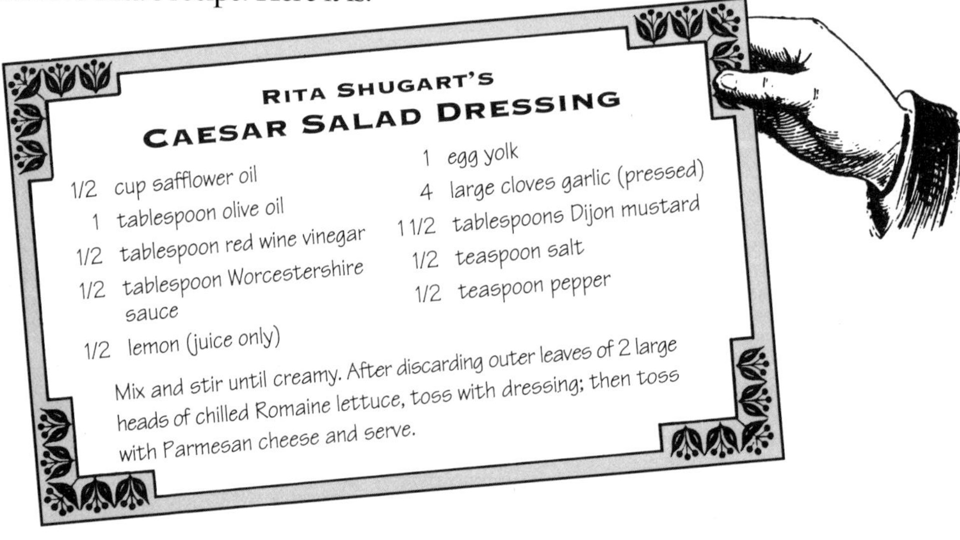

RITA SHUGART'S
CAESAR SALAD DRESSING

- 1/2 cup safflower oil
- 1 tablespoon olive oil
- 1/2 tablespoon red wine vinegar
- 1/2 tablespoon Worcestershire sauce
- 1/2 lemon (juice only)
- 1 egg yolk
- 4 large cloves garlic (pressed)
- 1 1/2 tablespoons Dijon mustard
- 1/2 teaspoon salt
- 1/2 teaspoon pepper

Mix and stir until creamy. After discarding outer leaves of 2 large heads of chilled Romaine lettuce, toss with dressing; then toss with Parmesan cheese and serve.

Spreading the Word

"And once sent out, a word takes wing irrevocably."
—Horace

One cliché I never want to read in a review is that Fandango is the "best-kept secret" in Pacific Grove—or, for that matter, the "best-kept secret" anywhere. I'm proud of Fandango, and I want the world to know about it.

I probably contribute most to Fandango from a public-relations standpoint. I refer a lot of people there. Seagate employees, Seagate customers, the vendors we buy from, investment bankers, and even competitors—just about anybody I come into contact with.

ONE SECRET FOR SUCCESS:
A WELL-STOCKED WINE CELLAR.

Rita does the same with customers at her store, as well as with people she meets in the world of bridge. This is a tourist area, obviously, and people from around the country—and around the world—like to vacation here. When I find out that anybody I deal with is coming here, I steer them to Fandango.

I enjoy promoting the restaurant, and I've had some pleasant surprises when wearing my P.R. hat. Not long ago I was having a business dinner in Minneapolis with an executive of a computer company. As we were getting to know each other, I mentioned that I owned half of the finest restaurant on the Monterey Peninsula.

"Oh," he said, "Fandango."

It turned out he spends several days a month in San Jose and often comes down to the Monterey Peninsula and dines at Fandango.

PIERRE ON FANDANGO'S CLIENTELE

If you are on a budget, you do not have to spend a lot of money here. There is a wide choice of entrees at very reasonable prices, and a broad choice of wines at a reasonable price. But should you wish to indulge in more expensive fare, we offer that in both culinary fare and wine. We cover the spectrum, if you will.

ATMOSPHERE

"There is material enough in a single flower for the ornament of a score of cathedrals."

—JOHN RUSKIN

Flowers—inside and outside—are a key ingredient in Fandango's atmosphere. Marietta handles the flower arrangements inside the restaurant. She has a wonderful touch. She started arranging flowers when she was in high school. Later she polished her skills at The Old House restaurant in Monterey, where she arranged flowers once a week.

"There's no one thing that makes a restaurant succeed, but thousands of things that come together—and it works or it doesn't."

—MARIETTA BAIN

It was as much a treat for her as it was a job. She loves flowers, and The Old House had a big budget for them.

Not only did she sharpen her skills in flower arranging, she learned a lot about purchasing flowers in volume. That's important when you're buying as many flowers as we buy at Fandango.

She usually gets the flowers on Thursday and does about sixty vases for the restaurant, plus flowers for the two bars and the upstairs and downstairs bathrooms.

FRED WUTHRICH, THE GARDENER.

The flowers outside are cared for by gardener Fred Wuthrich, who's a real plus for the restaurant.

Pierre and Marietta met him when they bought their Monterey home. One of the things that attracted them to it was its beautiful garden, which Fred maintained.

As Marietta says, "He's a professional. A full-time gardener—not a gardener and something else. When customers come to Fandango—before they even get to the door—they see his work. We want them to think, 'The people who own this restaurant really like being here.'"

A People Place

"People have one thing in common: They are all different."
—Robert Zend

Well, we do like being here, and we like being a little out of the ordinary. Whatever we are, we're definitely not conformists. And neither are our customers.

Someone once asked me: "What's the dress code at Fandango?"

I said, "Anything from T-shirt to tux."

Which about covers it.

The point is, we want people to feel comfortable and have fun at Fandango. You really do see T-shirts and tuxedos here, and it doesn't seem to bother our customers. In fact, it's attracted a really good cross-section of people.

That mix is part of Fandango's atmosphere. You can't write down what makes it work. Like the corporate culture at Seagate Technology, its atmosphere is indefinable. But I tell people what its end result is: fun, enjoyment, more good vibes than bad vibes.

Most important to the atmosphere is the people—both our staff and our customers. You'll see visitors from around the world at Fandango. You'll see your neighbors here, and celebrities too.

(Some of our neighbors who come here—Hank Ketcham, for instance—are pretty well known.)

The nice thing is, Fandango isn't a place for gawkers or autograph hounds. People who come here know they can relax, have fun, and not be hassled.

That doesn't mean they won't be recognized.

Arnold Palmer once came in for dinner during the AT&T. One of our regular customers—an avid golfer—was seated two tables away. He'd just finished his own dinner, but he lingered over coffee. He kept his distance, but eyed the golfing legend closely. Finally, when he'd seemingly had his fill of coffee and Arnold's aura, he left.

The next night, he returned to Fandango. He didn't bother with the menu. As soon as he was seated, he told the waiter, "I'll have the lamb shank and fettucini pasta. It's

"The couscous is sensational—the onion soup too. And all their meat dishes are excellent. Besides the wonderful food, it's the ambience, the welcome you get, the service, and the general feel of the place—all of it sparked by Pierre's presence. It's one of our favorite restaurants."

—Hank Ketcham

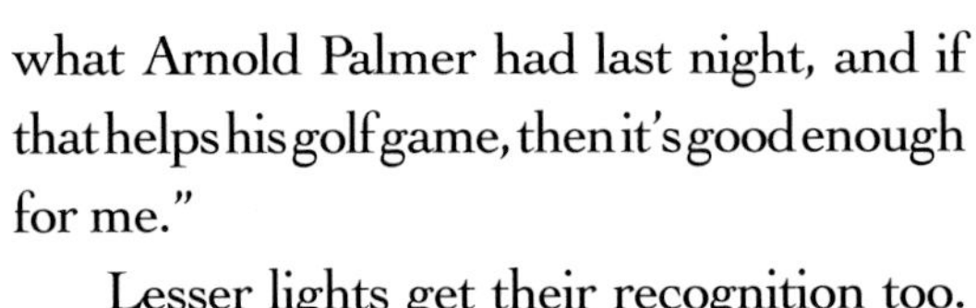

what Arnold Palmer had last night, and if that helps his golf game, then it's good enough for me."

Lesser lights get their recognition too. Rita and I were having dinner here a few years back in the middle of Salinas Rodeo Week. We noticed a young man passing by our table dressed in new Levis, a fancy, yoked, cowboy shirt, and a new cowboy hat. He could have been a tourist, duded up for the rodeo. But from his weathered look and the gingerly way he eased himself into the chair—as though favoring an aching body—we figured he was the real McCoy.

After the waiter brought him a menu, he took out his wallet and began counting his money, apparently checking his resources against our prices. Rita and I guessed that whatever bumps and bruises he'd picked up at the rodeo, they hadn't netted him much prize money.

Rita called the waiter over and told him she'd pick up the tab, but to tell the cowboy to order whatever he wanted—that it was a special that Fandango sometimes offered to rodeo cowboys.

Once the waiter convinced him that the offer was genuine, the cowboy ordered a steak dinner and tore into it with gusto. We like to think it gave him a boost for another day of riding and roping.

WE HUNG THIS ENDORSEMENT NEXT TO OUR FRONT DOOR.

No Place Like It

"The Fandango is fast, and can sometimes become furious."
—Mary Clark & Clement Crisp, The History of Dance

It has been almost twenty years since I started seriously considering the restaurant business. My initial interest was sparked by my love for the warmth and camaraderie you'd find in an English pub.

Along the way I had images of fancier establishments—elegant places, where the napery was fine linen and the fare was *haute cuisine.*

And then my good friend Pierre—a guy who knew what he was doing—introduced me to Fandango.

I resisted at first, until finally I realized that the restaurant of his dreams was not much different from the one I dreamed about. A comfortable place, where an international golfing legend or a local duffer, an Indy 500 winner or a Fortune 500 executive, a Monterey Peninsula resident or a transient cowpoke, could all have a good meal and a good time—and feel at home.

I think we've achieved our dream.

Life at Fandango—like the dance it was named for—is sometimes fast, and often furious. But most important—it's always fun.

That's why we're here.

And now that I've got that out of the way, I think it's time we all sat down together and had a bite to eat:

FANDANGO FARE

Cooking is an art, not a science. A recipe for a dish can list the ingredients and tell the means, sequence, and time of preparation. But when all is said and done, your Pasta Puttanesca is probably going to end up tasting different from mine.

Maybe your tomatoes are sweeter. Maybe my anchovies are saltier. Maybe I heap my tablespoons. Maybe you level yours.

It doesn't matter. Recipes aren't exact, technical specifications; they're guidelines.

If you don't have Cajun sausage for your Spanish Omelette, try Polish sausage instead. If you don't have wasabi for your Oriental Chicken Salad, try a little Dijon mustard. Substitute ingredients, do without them, and—if you think they'll improve your dish—add some of your own. Above all, don't be intimidated by the recipe. When you're in the kitchen, you're in command.

The enjoyment of a meal is subjective, determined to a great extent by the atmosphere. I don't imagine your home looks like our restaurant. Still, if you want to duplicate the Fandango experience, I can offer you a hint: Whatever dish you choose, prepare it and serve it with love.

And have a good time doing it.

Cheese Blintzes

"A man can forget absolutely everything—except to eat."
—Jewish Folk Saying

Blintz comes from a Yiddish word, *blintze,* which comes from a Russian word, *blinyets,* meaning little pancake. And basically that's what they are: little pancakes—or crepes—filled with a cream cheese topping.

THE PANCAKE

- 2/3 cup flour
- 1 1/2 cups milk
- 4 eggs
- 1 pinch salt
- 1 dash vanilla extract

Combine the flour and salt in one bowl; combine the milk and eggs in another. Then gradually add the egg-and-milk mixture to the salt-and-flour mixture. Add vanilla extract and beat the new mixture thoroughly to prevent lumping. Cover and chill for about 30 minutes.

Pour about 3 tablespoons of batter on a medium hot, lightly buttered griddle and rotate to form an 8-inch pancake. Fry until the batter sets and curls at the edges.

Tip it out onto a clean cloth, fried-side up. Your batter should make about 16 blintzes.

THE FILLING

- 1/2 pound cottage cheese
- 3/4 pounds cream cheese
- 1 egg
- 1/4 cup sugar
- 1 ounce Grand Marnier
- 1 pinch cinnamon
- 1 pinch salt
- 1 pinch grated orange rind

Mix the ingredients well and place a heaping tablespoon of the mixture in the center of each pancake. Fold in the edges and roll the pancakes into tubes.

Then bake them until they're warmed throughout. Delicious with sour cream and preserves.

Serves 4

Champagne goes well with these brunch dishes. You might also try a Mimosa: 3 parts chilled champagne to 1 part freshly squeezed orange juice.

Belgian Waffles

"Waffles, which have a very long history, are often mentioned in the poems of the end of the twelfth century."
—PROSPER MONTAGNÉ

It might work in French. The only rhyme in English I can think of for "waffle" is "awful," which Fandango's waffles definitely aren't.

It's enough to baffle you.

- 2 eggs
- 1 cup of milk
- 3 tablespoons salad oil
- 1 1/2 cups flour
- 3 teaspoons baking powder
- 4 teaspoons sugar
- 1 pinch salt

Mix the eggs, milk, and oil in a large bowl. Add the flour, baking powder, sugar, and salt, and stir until blended. That's your basic waffle batter. You can kick it up by adding cinnamon, nutmeg, coriander—whatever sounds good to you. It will make delicious waffles, though, just as is.

Pour enough of the batter onto a heated waffle iron to fill it. Close the iron and keep it closed until no more steam escapes. Open it and you should have a crisp, golden brown waffle. (You may want to oil the iron between waffles.) Butter, maple syrup, preserves, yogurt, ice cream, and so on, all make good toppings—but I'm sure you already know that.

Serves 4

French Toast

"Bread is the staff of life."
—JONATHAN SWIFT

It should come as no surprise that the French don't call this breakfast and brunch favorite French Toast. They sometime refer to it as *pain d'or*—golden bread—because of its color. In French households they also call it *pain perdu*—lost bread—because it's made from leftover bread from the day before.

At Fandango we use fresh bread for our French toast; not because day-old bread wouldn't work, but because there's no way to know how much leftover bread there'd be each morning.

- 8 thick slices of egg bread
- 4 eggs, slightly beaten
- 1 1/4 cups milk
- 2 1/2 tablespoons sugar
- 1 pinch cinnamon
- 1 dash vanilla extract

When you've mixed all the ingredients except the bread in a pan or baking dish, soak the slices of bread in the mixture, turning them so that both sides get saturated. Brown them on each side in a buttered, hot skillet or pan.

Serves 4

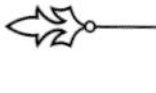

Spanish Omelette

"There is no such thing as a pretty good omelette."
—French Proverb

This is the way to make a *very* good omelette. It's an open-faced omelette, and it looks as good as it tastes.

- 3 eggs
- 1 tablespoon butter
- 5 slices Cajun sausage, cut on diagonal
- 2 tablespoons green onion, chopped
- 2 tablespoons white onion, chopped
- 2 tablespoons mild Ortega chili
- 2-3 slices cheddar cheese
- 1 cup shredded iceberg lettuce
- 2 tablespoons guacamole
- 2 tablespoons hot salsa
- 1 tablespoons sour cream

Beat eggs with a pinch of salt. Heat a skillet to medium-high and add butter. When butter foams, add eggs, swirling the pan as they set. When the omelette is almost firm, lay sausage slices on top in a star pattern. Add salsa and sprinkle onions on the omelette. Add the cheese to the center of the omelette. Add the Ortega chile. Remove pan from heat and put under broiler until cheese is melted. Remove and slide omelette onto a plate. Cover a third of the omelette with lettuce. Put the guacamole and sour cream side by side on top of the lettuce. Garnish with parsley and serve.

Serves 1

RECOMMENDED WINES
Sangria

Croque Monsieur Soufflé

"Everything in a pig is good. What ingratitude has permitted his name to become a term of opprobrium?"
—Grimod De La Reynière

THE SANDWICH

- 2 slices white bread
- 2 pieces thinly sliced ham
- 2 pieces thinly sliced Swiss cheese

Place the 2 slices of ham between the 2 slices of cheese, then put it all between the 2 slices of bread. In other words, make a ham and cheese sandwich. Then trim the crusts from the bread.

THE SAUCE

- 2 egg yolks
- 4 ounces shredded Swiss cheese
- 2 ounces whipping cream
- salt and pepper

Put egg yolks, cheese, and whipping cream in a bowl and mix with a rubber spatula.

Put the sandwich in a pan and pour mixture over it. Bake at 325°F. for 10 to 15 minutes, or until the cheese turns golden.

Serves 1

RECOMMENDED WINES
Pinot Blanc, Gewürztraminer, Pinot Noir

Eggs Benedict

"Nothing helps scenery like ham and eggs."
—MARK TWAIN

I like the traditional ham or Canadian bacon with this dish, but the smoked salmon is a nice variation. Back East they refer to that version as Eggs Nova Scotia. I suppose we could call it Eggs Monterey Bay.

1 English muffin

2 eggs

2 slices ham, Canadian bacon, or smoked salmon

Toast and butter muffin halves. Cover with ham, Canadian bacon, or smoked salmon, which can be warm or cold. Poach eggs and place on muffin halves.

BLENDER HOLLANDAISE SAUCE

1 stick butter

3 large egg yolks

1 tablespoon lemon juice

1 pinch cayenne

Melt the butter in a small, heavy saucepan.

Combine egg yolks, lemon juice, and cayenne in a blender. Cover the blender and switch it on and off quickly several times. Remove the cover, turn the blender to high, and gradually add the melted butter. Cover blender and let it run for about a minute. Turn off for about half a minute. Repeat until sauce thickens and peaks. Pour sauce over the eggs and serve.

Serves 1

RECOMMENDED WINES
Champagne, Mimosa

Velouté Bongo Bongo

"Oysters are amatory food."

—Lord Byron

This recipe originated with Trader Vic. Basil (Bill) Coleman—an executive with Trader Vic's for twenty-five years before becoming general manager at The Lodge at Pebble Beach—passed it on to Pierre. It was a great favorite at Club XIX for many years and is very popular at Fandango today.

1 1/2 quarts clam juice
3 bunches cleaned spinach
1 jar Pacific oysters
1 small onion, chopped
2 cloves garlic, chopped
1/2 cup oyster sauce
1 cup white wine
2 tablespoons brandy
1 pinch each, tarragon, thyme, basil
1/2 bay leaf
1/2 cup whipped cream

Sauté onion and garlic until they're limp. Add oysters, white wine, brandy and spices. Cook about 10 minutes. In a separate soup pot boil the clam juice and spinach. Add oyster mixture and oyster sauce and bring to a boil. Add salt and pepper to taste. Put all in a blender and puree. Float whipped cream and glaze under the broiler.

Serves 6

RECOMMENDED WINES

Gerwürztraminer, Riesling, Vouvray

Basque Salad

"The greatest dishes are very simple dishes."
—AUGUSTE ESCOFFIER

For simple pleasure, it's hard to beat this Basque Salad. Although it's easy to prepare, its flavors are complex. Is it the raspberry vinaigrette combining with the bleu cheese that makes it so distinctive? Or is it the interaction of the tomatoes and oranges? Maybe it's the mingling of spinach leaves and walnut that does it.

Who knows? It's as mysterious as the Basque language itself. The bottom line: It's delicious.

- 2 bunches fresh cleaned spinach
- 2 oranges, sectioned
- 2 tomatoes, chopped in large pieces
- 1 cup bleu cheese
- 1/2 cup walnuts
- 4 tablespoons raspberry vinaigrette
- 1 hard-boiled egg, quartered

Tear the spinach and line the individual service dishes with it. Add the tomato pieces, walnuts, and bleu cheese, garnish with orange sections and egg quarters, and sprinkle with raspberry vinaigrette. (To make raspberry vinaigrette, just add a dash or two of raspberry vinegar to the vinaigrette recipe on page 65.)

Serves 4

RECOMMENDED WINES

Gewürztraminer, Riesling, fruity Chardonnay

CALIFORNIA
Sauvignon Blanc

Salad Niçoise

"Oh, green and glorious! Oh, herbacious treat! 'Twould tempt the dying anchorite to eat: Back to the world he'd turn his fleeting soul, And plunge his fingers in the salad bowl!"

—SIDNEY SMITH, FROM RECIPE FOR A SALAD

This is definitely an herbacious treat—although pure vegetarians will shun the fish and eggs in it. It makes a great hot-weather meal.

- 1 head butter lettuce or red-leaf lettuce washed and drained
- 2 medium tomatoes, quartered
- 1/3 green bell pepper, cut in 1/4" strips
- 1/3 sweet yellow bell pepper, cut in 1/4" strips
- 1/3 sweet red bell pepper, cut in 1/4" strips
- 1 heart of celery diced
- 1/2 cucumber, peeled and sliced
- 3 green onions, chopped
- 1 red onion, sliced into rings
- 1 medium potato, boiled and diced in 1/2" cubes
- 1 cup cooked string beans
- 1 cup cooked garbanzo beans
- 1 cup canned albacore, drained, (preferably water packed)
- 9 anchovy filets
- 1/2 cup Niçoise olives (tiny black olives, packed in brine, not oil)
- 3 hard-boiled eggs, quartered lengthwise
- vinaigrette
- several fresh basil leaves, chopped

Arrange the lettuce leaves around a salad bowl and place the tomato quarters on top of them. Arrange the bell peppers, celery, cucumber, potatoes, and green beans on top of the tomatoes. Sprinkle the tuna and chopped basil on top of vegetables. Top each salad with 1 or 2 anchovy filets, 2 egg quarters, a few olives, and green onions. Dress the salad with 1 cup of vinaigrette immediately before serving and toss lightly.

Serves 6

VINAIGRETTE

- 1 cup red wine vinegar
- 2 teaspoons Dijon mustard
- 2 teaspoons shallots, chopped
- 1 clove garlic, finely chopped
- 2 teaspoons parsley, chopped
- 1 teaspoon capers (optional)
- 1 teaspoon fresh basil, chopped
- 1 dash Worcestershire sauce
- 2 cups extra virgin olive oil
- 2 cups vegetable oil

Mix all the ingredients, except the oils. Then combine the oils and blend them in with the other ingredients. Store in refrigerator until needed.

RECOMMENDED WINES

Dry Rosé, Sauvignon Blanc, Rosé de Provence

Chicken Salad Oriental

"Oh, East is East, and West is West, and never the twain shall meet,
Till Earth and Sky stand presently at God's great Judgment Seat."
—RUDYARD KIPLING

Kipling overstated the case. Try this East-West combination, and I bet you'll agree with me.

- 3 grilled boneless chicken breasts, skinned and sliced
- 1/2 cup sautéed sliced mushrooms
- 6 green onions, chopped
- 6 radishes, sliced
- 6 ripe cherry tomatoes, halved
- 18 black olives
- 3 hard-boiled eggs, halved
- 3 carrots, julienned
- 1 red and 1 green bell pepper, sliced
- 2 heads of iceberg lettuce
- 2 ounces sliced pickled ginger
- 1 package Oriental Rice Stick noodles, cooked per package instructions
- Oriental Dressing
- 3 tablespoons toasted sesame seeds
- 3 tablespoons toasted sliced almonds

ORIENTAL DRESSING

- 1/4 cup soy sauce
- 1 whole egg, raw
- 1/2 teaspoon sugar, superfine
- 1/4 tablespoon wasabi powder
- 1 dash cayenne
- 1/8 teaspoon dry mustard
- 1/4 cup sesame oil
- 1/4 cup safflower oil
- 1/4 cup rice vinegar
- 1 teaspoon fresh ginger juice (press sliced ginger root in garlic press for juice)

Mix all ingredients and blend well.

Line each serving dish with shredded lettuce and noodles, then arrange vegetables, egg half, and olives. Place the sliced chicken on top. Add Oriental Dressing, sesame seeds, and toasted almonds.

Then give your regrets to Rudyard and dig into this delicious East-sWest concoction.

Serves 6

RECOMMENDED WINES
Riesling, Rosé de Provence

Steamed Vegetable Plate

"There are only two or three things in life I don't like—but they're not vegetables."

—VICTOR RENAUD (CHEVALIER, ORDER OF AGRICULTURAL MERIT)

There's a barbecue restaurant about twenty minutes north of Fandango that calls itself "a vegetarian's nightmare." Although we feature many meat dishes, we're not that carnivorous.

If you're in the mood for a meatless repast, this is a good way to go:

- 1 artichoke
- 1 medium carrot, quartered
- 3 small white potatoes
- 1 small yellow squash, cut in thirds
- 2 whites of leek
- 3 medium mushrooms, sliced
- 6 asparagus tips
- 1 tomato Provençal

Prepare the vegetables and cook them in a steamer as follows:

Steam the artichoke separately for about 15 to 20 minutes, depending on its size. Remove it from steamer and keep it warm.

Next, steam the carrots and potatoes 10 to 15 minutes until they're fork tender. Remove them and keep them warm.

Add water to the steamer if necessary and add the squash, whites of leek, mushrooms, and asparagus tips.

TOMATO PROVENÇAL

Cut a ripe tomato in half and place 1 piece cut-side up in a thick-bottomed skillet coated with heated olive oil. Cook over high heat for 10 minutes. Turn the half over and cook 5 minutes more. Turn it cut-side up again and sprinkle it with a mixture of 1/4 cup of fine bread crumbs, 2 tablespoons parsley, and 1/2 teaspoon garlic, both finely chopped. Salt and pepper to taste and brown briefly under broiler.

Put the artichoke in the center of the plate and arrange the other vegetables around it. This is good with a lemon-butter sauce or with garlic mayonnaise on the side.

Serves 1

Fettuccine Primavera

"No man is lonely while eating spaghetti—
it requires so much attention."
—CHRISTOPHER MORLEY

The Italian word for springtime is *primavera*, but this preparation of pasta and fresh vegetables with cream sauce is good any time of year.

- 1 pound fettuccine, cooked *al dente*
- 1 tablespoon butter
- 1 clove garlic
- 4 shallots
- 1 cup of whipping cream
- 2 cups green peas
- 3 green onions, minced
- 2 medium carrots, shredded
- 2 medium zucchini, julienned
- 2 medium yellow squash, julienned
- 1 cup broccoli buds
- 2 large tomatoes, peeled and chopped
- 2 tablespoons grated Parmesan cheese

Sauté the garlic and shallots in butter until limp, then pour in the whipping cream. Stir as you add blanched vegetables: peas, green onions, carrots, zucchini, yellow squash, and broccoli. Cook briefly over medium heat. Pour the primavera sauce over the fettuccine, garnish with tomato, and sprinkle with Parmesan cheese.

Serves 4

RECOMMENDED WINES

Pinot Blanc, Sauvignon Blanc, Gewürztraminer

Pasta Puttanesca

"Everything you see, I owe to spaghetti."
—Sophia Loren

This classic dish originated long ago in the Trastevere district of Rome, which was a hangout for *puttane*—prostitutes. The sauce is good with just about any type of pasta.

Cook 1 pound of pasta *al dente.*
While it's cooking, sauté:

- 2 tablespoons extra virgin olive oil
- 2 cloves garlic, peeled and chopped
- 2 ounces shallots, chopped

Add:

- 1 teaspoon capers
- 1/2 cup pitted kalamata olives
- 1 1/2 cups diced fresh tomatoes
- 1/2 teaspoon pesto (optional)
- 8 chopped anchovy filets

At the very end add 5 or 6 fresh shredded basil leaves and sauté for a few seconds. Then serve the sauce over the pasta. A great quickie meal.

Serves 4

RECOMMENDED WINES
Chianti Classico, Barolo, Zinfandel

Canneloni Niçoise

"Pasta is the food—if not of love—certainly of close companionship."

—ANNA DEL CONTE FROM PORTRAIT OF PASTA

Canneloni, in Italian, means "big pipes," and that's what these tubes of pasta are. Over the centuries, Nice felt the impact of invaders from north, south, east, and west; consequently the Niçoise cuisine is eclectic. Although the canneloni is Italian, the dish has been prepared in Nice for so long it merits the title Canneloni Niçoise.

FILLING

1 pound cleaned fresh spinach
1/2 pound cooked meat (daube, roasted pork, veal, or chicken)
1 cup cooked rice (optional)
1 onion, chopped
1 cup Swiss cheese, grated
1/2 cup Parmesan cheese, grated
1 egg yolk
2 tablespoons olive oil
salt and pepper

Cook spinach in salted water for about 2 minutes. Drain and squeeze out all the water. Cook onion in 1 tablespoon olive oil until it's transparent.

Grind spinach, onion, meat, and rice in a meat grinder. Mix ground ingredients with egg, salt, pepper, and the rest of the olive oil.

PASTA

Cut thin pasta sheets in 4-inch by 3-inch rectangles. Cook them for 1 minute in a pot of boiling, salted water, and then lay them out on a towel to dry.

TOMATO SAUCE

2 pounds tomatoes, very ripe, quartered
1 onion, chopped
2 teaspoons tomato paste
3 strips bacon (chopped)
3 tablespoons olive oil
2 cloves of garlic, chopped
1 bouquet garni (8 stems of parsley, 1 bay leaf, 3 stems of thyme, tied together)
1 pinch sugar
salt and pepper

Sauté the onion and bacon in olive oil, cooking very slowly for 10 minutes. Add the tomatoes, tomato paste, and bouquet garni, and cook covered for 45 minutes.

Add garlic, salt, pepper, and sugar, and cook for another 10 minutes, then remove from heat.

ASSEMBLY

Place 3 to 5 tablespoons of stuffing on the pasta squares and roll them up into "big pipes"—canneloni. Arrange the pasta rolls in a gratin dish and spoon some tomato sauce over them. Sprinkle both Parmesan and Swiss cheese over the canneloni and bake slowly until the cheese is browned.

Serves 4

RECOMMENDED WINES

Côtes de Provence Rouge, Côtes du Rhone, Sauvignon Blanc

Paella Fandango

"La mejor salsa del mundo es el hambre."
(The best sauce in the world is hunger.)
—MIGUEL DE CERVANTES

If you asked people outside Spain what's the most typical Spanish dish, the majority would probably say, "Paella."

This delicious dish gets its name from the special metal pan that the cooks of Valencia use to prepare rice dishes. If you don't have a paella pan, you can use a large skillet or a wok—and you can still call the finished product paella. Why not? You're the cook.

- 1/2 cup olive oil
- 1 large onion, chopped
- 2 cloves garlic, chopped
- 2 large tomatoes, diced
- 2 bell peppers, 1 red, 1 yellow (you can substitute green for either), cut in strips
- 2 cups of white rice
- 8 cups of chicken broth
- 3 tablespoons of chopped parsley
- 2 large pinches of saffron threads
- 2 chicken breasts (each cut in 4-5 pieces)
- 1 chorizo sausage (about 1/2 pound), cut in 1/2-inch slices
- 1/2 pound of scallops
- 1/2 pound of calamari
- 1/2 pound of shrimp, peeled, tails intact
- 8-10 little-neck clams
- 8-10 mussels
- 1 cup peas, fresh or frozen
- salt, pepper, cayenne

In a skillet heat olive oil and add onion, garlic, tomatoes, and bell pepper strips. Sauté until limp. Add white rice and chicken broth and bring to a boil. Add the chopped parsley and the saffron threads and cook for 20 minutes at a simmer. Add the remaining ingredients and cook to doneness, probably about 20 to 40 minutes. You're the cook (see above) so you decide. Season to taste with salt, pepper, and cayenne and serve.

Serves 8

RECOMMENDED WINES
Rioja, Zinfandel, Côtes du Rhone

CUVÉE
1989
Ott*
COTES DE PROVENCE
CÔTES DE PROVENCE
Domaines
STILL WHITE
CLOS MIREILLE

Fresh Petrale Sole

"Fish dinner will make a man spring like a flea."
—THOMAS JORDAN

At one time, when you ordered filet of sole in a restaurant you got European Sole *(Solea solea)*. Nowadays the term can refer to any flatfish, from flounder to halibut. We serve a local favorite, Petrale sole *(Eopsetta jordani)*. They can be found from the Bering Sea to Baja, but they're particularly at home in Monterey Bay.

In the early part of the century, the fish was prized by Chinese fishermen who lived near what is now Cannery Row. They'd dry them by stringing them on frames set on the roofs of their houses. What they didn't eat themselves, they'd export to China.

We serve them fresh at Fandango. And no matter what you call them—sole, flounder, or *Eopsetta jordani*—they're flat-out delectable.

THE FISH

For starters, dredge a 1/2-inch-thick filet of Petrale sole in flour. Then sauté in butter for about 3 minutes on one side and 1 1/2 minutes on the other.

THE SAUCE

- 1/2 teaspoon finely chopped shallots
- 1/2 lemon (juice only)
- 1 ounce white wine
- 4 teaspoons chopped parsley
- 1 tablespoon butter
- salt and pepper

Sauté shallots in butter until translucent. Add white wine, lemon juice, and chopped parsley. Bring to boil and reduce to half.

As soon as the filet is sautéed, cover it with sauce and garnish it with parsley.

Serves 1

RECOMMENDED WINES
Chardonnay, White Rioja, Sancerre

Scampi Basquaise

Asko Dakik Bizitxen Baldin Ba dakik.
(You know much if you know how to live.)
—BASQUE PROVERB

The Basques crisscross the Pyrennees, moving between the French and Spanish cultures with ease as they cling to their own proud traditions. Their cooking—like their character—is honest and direct. This recipe would be delicious in any culture.

- 32 prawns (16-20 count per pound), shelled, deveined
- 4 shallots, chopped
- 1/2 cup chopped onion
- 1/2 cup chopped scallions
- 1 large tomato, diced
- 1/2 teaspoon chopped garlic
- 3 bunches spinach leaves
- 10 ounces white wine
- 1/2 lemon (juice only)
- 1 ounce raspberry vinegar
- 6 ounces butter
- salt, pepper, and cayenne pepper to taste

Heat butter in skillet. Briefly sauté shallots, onion, scallions, garlic, tomato, and prawns. Add spinach, white wine, lemon juice, and raspberry vinegar. Season with salt, pepper, and cayenne. Bring to a boil and serve over either saffron rice or spaghettini.

Serves 4

RECOMMENDED WINES
Sauvignon Blanc, Pinot Blanc

Lobster Tail

"Seeing is deceiving. It's eating that's believing."
—JAMES THURBER

If there's any creature in the world that tastes better than it looks, it has to be the lobster. I acknowledge the bravery of the first person who ever ate an oyster. Still, if I were giving out an award for culinary courage, I'd pin in it on the first person who ever ate a lobster.

Whoever did it set a great precedent.

- 1 lobster tail, 10-14 ounces or larger
- 2 ounces white wine
- 1/2 lemon (juice only)
- 3 ounces soft butter
- 1/4 teaspoon paprika
- 1/4 teaspoon salt
- 1 pinch each white pepper, cayenne pepper
- 1 ounce melted butter (for dunking)

Lay the lobster tail on a cutting board with the top side up. With a sharp knife, split the shell lengthwise up the middle, at the same time butterflying the meat. Separate the meat from the shell, leaving the end attached. Lay the butterflied meat over the top of the shell, coat it with soft butter, sprinkle with lemon juice and white wine and season with paprika, salt, and pepper. Place under broiler 10 to 12 minutes or put in a hot oven (425°F.) for 10 to12 minutes.

This is good with a side dish of melted butter for dunking.

Serves 1

RECOMMENDED WINES

Pinot Blanc, Chardonnay, Chablis Grand Crû

CALIFORNIA
Cabernet Sauvignon

Chicken Mediterranean

"Poultry is for the cook what canvas is for the painter."

—JEAN ANTHELME BRILLAT-SAVARIN

- 1 fryer, cut up
- 1 cup onion, chopped
- 1 cup celery, chopped
- 1 clove garlic, minced
- 10 cracked Italian olives
- 1 tablespoon capers
- 1 teaspoon sugar
- 1/2 cup white wine
- 1 piece fresh rosemary (1 1/2 inches), minced
- 1 teaspoon fine herbs
- 1/2 teaspoon basil
- 1 teaspoon Worcestershire sauce
- 1 1/2 cups chicken stock
- 1 teaspoon tomato paste
- 1 teaspoon wine vinegar

Sauté the chicken pieces in olive oil in a Dutch oven, then remove them and set them aside.

In the same pan, sauté the onions, celery, and garlic until they're limp. Add sugar, tomato paste, herbs, wine, vinegar and the rest of the ingredients. Cover and simmer for 15 minutes.

Add the pieces of chicken and simmer for 30 minutes.

Serves 4

RECOMMENDED WINES

Chardonnay, Chianti Classico, Beaujolais

Couscous Algérois

"Like aïoli and bouillabaisse, couscous is a spectacular creation, a feast in itself."

—MIREILLE JOHNSTON, FROM THE CUISINE OF THE SUN

As the name suggests, this dish originated in North Africa. It made its way to Comps-sur-Artuby in Provence, where—for more than 130 years—it's been a mainstay at the Hotel Bain.

- 1 pound lamb shank, cut in cubes
- 2 large carrots, cut in 1" pieces
- 2 medium zucchini, cut in 1" pieces
- 3 medium yellow squash, quartered
- 3 medium turnips, peeled and quartered
- 3 small artichoke hearts, cut in half
- 1/2 cup onion, chopped
- 2 tablespoons shallots, chopped
- 1 tablespoon garlic, chopped
- 1/2 cup parsley, chopped
- 1 tablespoon Four Spice (blend of cinnamon sticks, peppercorns, cloves, and cumin)
- 1/2 tablespoon red chili pepper (powder or ground)
- 1 tablespoon tomato paste
- 1 pinch each, thyme, basil, rosemary, marjoram, cayenne pepper, ground black pepper, salt
- 1 whole bay leaf
- 2 quarts lamb stock or chicken broth
- 1 cup red wine
- 1 cup white wine
- 1/2 cup olive oil
- harissa sauce (optional)

In a large, heavy, saucepan, sauté onion, shallots, garlic, and parsley in olive oil until translucent. Add lamb cubes and thyme, basil, rosemary, bay leaf, marjoram, cayenne, and black pepper, and sauté until meat is half cooked (about 15 minutes). Add carrots and turnips and cook for 7 minutes or until the carrots are half cooked, then add the Four Spice, ground red chili pepper, and tomato paste and cook over low heat for 5 minutes. Pour in the stock (heated), add wine and bring to boil. Add squash, zucchini, and artichoke and cook until the artichoke is tender (about 20 minutes).

Traditionally, couscous grain is steamed in a couscoussière—a kind of double boiler with a perforated upper pot. You can make a workable substitute, using a sieve lined with a linen towel in place of the perforated upper pot. But why not keep it simple?

This method makes wonderful couscous: Dissolve 2 tablespoons butter in 1 1/2 cups of boiling water and add 1 cup of couscous. Stir and cover, then take it off the heat and let it stand for 5 minutes. Before serving the couscous, fluff it with a fork. You can use broth instead of water to give the couscous a richer flavor.

Put the couscous on a plate. Put the vegetables and meat together in a bowl. Pour half the broth over the couscous, half in a bowl as a side dish. Dab harissa sauce on the couscous plate. Use caution—it's hot. (Try a side dish of raisins and toasted almonds with this.)

Serves 4.

RECOMMENDED WINES

Dry Rosé, Zinfandel, Côtes du Rhone

Rack of Lamb Provençal

"A man seldom thinks with more earnestness of anything than he does of his dinner."

—SAMUEL JOHNSON

This is a serious dish. I've always loved lamb, but the sauce Pedro De La Cruz uses takes it to another level. The recipe has been in the Bain family for generations, and Pierre passed it on to Pedro.

THE LAMB

4 1 1/2-pound racks of lamb, trimmed and seasoned with *herbs de Provence*, salt, pepper, and rosemary.

Refrigerate overnight. Grill the racks over mesquite or fruitwood on a hot fire to sear, then move the meat away from direct heat, cooking at lower temperature to desired doneness.

THE LAMB SAUCE

1 tablespoon butter
1 shallot or small onion, chopped
1 large clove garlic, chopped
2 tablespoons flour
1/2 teaspoon tomato paste
1 1/4 cups concentrated lamb stock
1 ounce each: white wine, red wine
1 pinch each of salt, black pepper, thyme, bay leaf, whole sweet basil, rosemary
1 ounce cognac or brandy
2 tablespoons butter

Sauté the butter, garlic, and shallot until translucent. Stir constantly as you add the flour and then blend over low heat for 2 minutes. Add the tomato paste and cook 2 more minutes. Add lamb stock, wines, and spices and whisk until smooth; cook 15 minutes over low heat. Add cognac or brandy and cook 1 to 2 minutes.

Remove from heat, add butter, and whisk until well blended. Serve the sauce over the lamb.

Serves 4

RECOMMENDED WINES

Châteauneuf-du-Pape, Pinot Noir, Cabernet Sauvignon

1987
WINE IMPORTS, LTD.
CONTAINS SULFITES
PRODUCT OF FRANCE

Osso Bucco

"The discovery of a new dish does more for the happiness of mankind that the discovery of a new star."

—Anthelme Brillat-Savarin

This dish originated in Milan but found a home in Provence. It's characterized by an herbal mixture called a gremolata, without which—say the Milanese cooks—you can't have genuine osso bucco.

- 4 veal shanks
- 1 cup flour
- 1/2 cup olive oil
- 1 onion thinly sliced
- 4 leeks, whites only
- 1 bay leaf
- 2 cups small mushroom caps
- 2 carrots, quartered
- 4 yellow squash, quartered
- 1 stalk celery diced
- 6 new potatoes
- 1/2 cup dry white wine
- 2 1/2 cups tomatoes, chopped fresh, or canned Italian plum tomatoes
- 1 teaspoon tomato paste
- 1 1/2 teaspoons chopped parsley
- 1 clove garlic, crushed
- 1 tablespoon grated lemon peel
- salt, pepper

Dredge the shanks with flour and put them in a medium hot skillet with the olive oil. When they're browned, take them out and put the bay leaf and vegetables (except the tomatoes) in the skillet and cook over medium heat for 5 minutes. Add the wine and simmer until it evaporates. Add the shanks, the tomatoes, and tomato paste to the ingredients in the skillet. Cover the skillet and simmer until the shanks are tender, about 1 to 1 1/2 hours. You might need to add wine or water during this period.

Remove the shanks and strain the sauce.

Put the sauce and meat back in the pan and stir in the gremolata—that's the garlic, parsley, and lemon peel blended together. Salt and pepper to taste. Simmer for about 5 minutes and it's ready.

Serves 4

RECOMMENDED WINES

Chianti Classico, Barbaresco, Pinot Noir

Veal Shank Pot au Feu

"There warn't really anything the matter with [the food]...
only everything was cooked by itself. In a barrel of odds and ends it is different;
things get mixed up, and the juice kind of swaps around, and the things go better."

—MARK TWAIN, FROM THE ADVENTURES OF HUCKLEBERRY FINN

In this dish, certainly, "the juice kind of swaps around." It's a hearty meal with a lot of wonderful flavors.

- 4 veal shanks (about 1 pound each)
- 4 leeks (white part only), rinsed and trimmed
- 1 onion, peeled and halved (studded with 1 clove each)
- 2 carrots, peeled, quartered, and halved
- 2 turnips, peeled and quartered
- 12 mushroom heads, rinsed
- 1/2 cup vegetable oil
- 1 pint white wine
- 1/2 cup sherry, medium dry
- 1 bouquet garni (8 stems of parsley, 1 bay leaf, 3 stems of thyme, tied together)
- 2 cloves
- salt, black or white pepper corn

Brown the veal shanks in oil. It should take about 10 minutes. Then put them in a heavy pot and cover them with cold water, adding salt, pepper, onion, and bouquet garni. Bring the liquid to a simmer (don't boil). Cook uncovered for 30 minutes, skimming the foam and impurities.

After 30 minutes, cover and put in a medium hot oven (just enough for the broth to simmer) for 45 minutes. Add the leeks and cook for 15 minutes. Add the potatoes and cook for another 15 minutes. Add the rest of the vegetables, sherry, white wine, and cook for 15 minutes, or until vegetables are done. Discard the onion and the bouquet garni.

Put the shanks on a platter and surround them with the vegetables. Then pour the broth over the pot au feu and serve.

Serve with cornichons, Dijon mustard, and horseradish.

Serves 4

RECOMMENDED WINES
Merlot, Pinot Noir

Porterhouse Steak

"I never see any home cooking. All I get is the fancy stuff."
—DUKE OF EDINBURGH

This is pretty close to home cooking.

At Fandango we put the steaks on our mesquite grill and then add a little salt, a little pepper, and a swipe or so of our Café de Paris Butter. (The butter's a little fancy, but not too fancy.)

CAFÉ DE PARIS BUTTER

- 8 ounces soft butter
- 1 teaspoon chopped parsley
- 1 1/2 teaspoons Dijon mustard
- 4 teaspoons tomato ketchup
- 1 teaspoon finely chopped garlic
- 1 teaspoon finely chopped shallots
- 1/2 teaspoon paprika
- 4 drops Worcestershire sauce
- 3 drops Tabasco sauce
- 1 pinch cayenne pepper
- salt and pepper to taste

Combine all the ingredients in a bowl, whisk until blended. Roll in parchment paper, and place in either the refrigerator or freezer until hard.

RECOMMENDED WINES

Cabernet Sauvignon, Côte Rotie, Barolo

Domaine
Les Pallières
S.C.E.A.

Sangria

Prix-Fixe Dinner

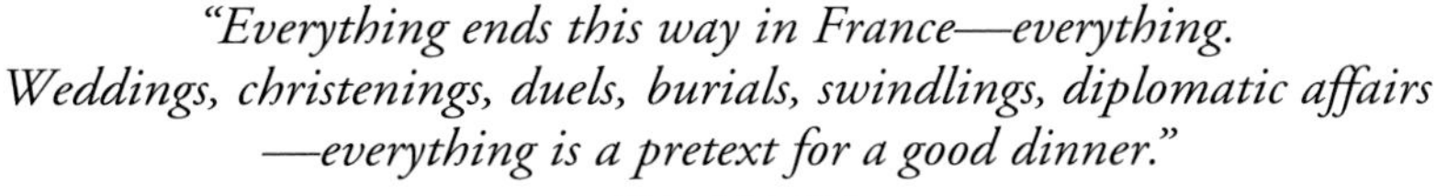

"Everything ends this way in France—everything. Weddings, christenings, duels, burials, swindlings, diplomatic affairs —everything is a pretext for a good dinner."

—Jean Anouilh

Tapas

Tapas are the Spanish versions of hors d'oeuvres. The word *tapa* means cover or lid. In the nineteenth century when stage coaches pulled into inns in southern Spain for a change of horses, the innkeepers would serve wine to the drivers and passengers. The changing of the teams could be hectic, so the innkeepers would cover the wine glasses with a slice of ham, cheese or bread to protect the wine from flies, dust, and whatever else might be floating about in the air. Thus, the little snacks became known as *tapas.*

That's one theory of how the word originated. Maybe it's true. Frankly, I don't think people would want flies, dust, or debris on their hors d'oeuvres any more than they'd want them in their wine.

Anyway, that's not a problem at Fandango.

Marinated Tricolor Bell Peppers

- 2 tablespoons olive oil
- 1 large red bell pepper, cut into 2-inch-wide strips
- 1 large yellow bell pepper, cut into 2-inch-wide strips
- 1 large green bell pepper, cut into 2-inch-wide strips
- 1 large onion halved lengthwise and cut into 2-inch-wide slices
- 1/4 cup white wine-vinegar
- 2 tablespoons minced fresh basil
- freshly ground white pepper
- salt

Heat the oil in a large skillet over medium heat. Add bell peppers and onion. Cover and cook until the peppers exude liquid and are slightly softened, about 5 minutes. Transfer to bowl. Add vinegar. Season with salt and pepper. Cover and refrigerate until well chilled. (You can prepare these a day ahead.)

Mix the basil with the white pepper and sprinkle over the bell peppers. Serve this either cold or at room temperature.

Serves 4

Pâté Maison

1	cup butter, divided
1	onion (small), chopped
1	teaspoon dry mustard
1/2	teaspoon salt
1/4	tablespoon curry powder
1/4	tablespoon ground cloves
1/8	tablespoon ground pepper
	dash cayenne
1	pound duckling liver (cleaned) or chicken liver
1	tablespoon unflavored gelatin
3	tablespoons water
1/2	cup whipping cream
2	tablespoons cognac or Madeira wine

Melt 1/4 cup of butter and add onion and spices. Cook and stir until the onion is tender and browned. Add the liver and cook until it's no longer pink. Put the liver and onion mixture into a food processor and blend until smooth.

Sprinkle the gelatin over the water and heat until it's dissolved.

Add the cream cognac and the remaining 3/4 cup of butter to the processor.

Add the gelatin mixture and process again until smooth. Refrigerate until ready to serve.

Serves 8 to 10

Tomato Soup

"Of soup and love, the first is best."

—SPANISH PROVERB

PART I

1 1/2	quarts chicken stock
1/2	quart tomato juice or 1 cup tomato sauce
1	leek (green part only)
1	celery stalk
3	whole ripe tomatoes, chopped
1	pinch each of thyme, sweet basil, whole oregano
1	bay leaf

Combine the above and bring to a boil and then let simmer for 5 minutes. Strain the mixture and set aside.

PART II

2	ounces of butter
1/2	medium onion, chopped
1	leek (white part only), chopped
1/2	teaspoon of chopped garlic
6	tablespoons of flour
2	teaspoons of tomato paste
1	teaspoon each of sugar, salt, and pepper

Melt the butter in a saucepan and add the chopped onion, leeks, and garlic. Cook until translucent. Add the flour and stir for 5 minutes. Add the tomato paste and cook over medium heat for 2 minutes. Combine the mixtures in a blender or with a whisk. Bring to a boil and add a teaspoon each of sugar, salt, and pepper. Simmer for 10 minutes. Strain and serve.

Serves 6 to 8

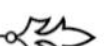

Fresh Salmon Filet

"A true gastronome should always be ready to eat, just as a soldier should always be ready to fight."
—CHARLES MONSELET

Cook the filet of salmon quickly over a hot grill—about 3 to 5 minutes, depending on its thickness—turning it when it's 2/3 done. Brush the salmon with lemon dill butter and serve it with grilled squash and string beans garnished with strips of red bell pepper.

LEMON DILL BUTTER

- 1/4 cup unsalted butter (room temperature)
- 1/2 lemon, juiced
- 1 tablespoon fresh dill, chopped

Mix together.

Serves 1

RECOMMENDED WINES
Chenin Blanc, Pinot Blanc, Beaujolais

Caramel Custard

THE CARAMEL

Basically this is simple syrup with a little heat added.

- 1/2 cup sugar
- 1/4 cup water

Boil the sugar and water in a small, heavy saucepan. When all the sugar is dissolved turn down heat to moderate and swirl the pan so that the mixture is in constant motion. When the mixture becomes caramel colored (about 5 to 10 minutes), carefully pour it into each of the custard cups, coating the sides and bottoms.

THE CUSTARD

- 2 cups milk (very hot)
- 1 vanilla bean split lengthwise
- 1/4 cup sugar
- 2 eggs
- 3 egg yolks

Beat the eggs and egg yolks into a blend. Stir in sugar. Add the vanilla to the milk and heat to almost boiling. Then pour into the egg blend very slowly, stirring constantly. Strain the mixture into the caramel-coated cups. Pour the custard into the individual cups and place them in a 300°F. oven in a shallow pan. Fill pan with 1 inch of hot water and bake for about 45 minutes to an hour, or until a knife inserted in the middle of the custard comes out clean. Chill the cups in the refrigerator for about 3 hours before serving.

Serves 4

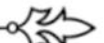

DESSERTS

"My advice to you is not to inquire why or whither,
but just enjoy your ice cream while it's on your plate—that's my philosophy."
—THORNTON WILDER

My philosophy isn't that far removed from Wilder's.
But who cares about philosophy now, anyway?
You've finished your vegetables: It's time for dessert.

Chocolate Mousse

1/2 pound semi-sweet chocolate
6 large eggs, separated
1/4 cup Grand Marnier
2 cups whipping cream
6 tablespoons sugar

Melt the chocolate over low heat, stirring it frequently to make sure it doesn't burn. When it's melted, remove it from the heat.

Put the egg yolks in a heavy-bottomed saucepan and put the pan over low heat. Beat the eggs with a wire whisk until they begin to thicken. Add the Grand Marnier and continue to beat until you have a uniform sauce. With a wooden spoon, stir the melted chocolate into the sauce until it's blended.

In another bowl, beat the whipping cream, adding the sugar as you go, until it's stiff. Then mix it in with the eggs, chocolate, and Grand Marnier.

Beat the egg whites until they're stiff, then fold them into the mixture.

Now you've got mousse. Spoon it into serving dishes and chill for at least 6 hours.

Serves 6

Vacherin Glacé Marquise

Too much of a good thing can be wonderful."

—MAE WEST

- 6 large scoops of vanilla ice cream
- 12 meringue shells
- hot chocolate sauce
- 3/4 cup sliced, toasted almonds
- 3 cups sweet whipped cream

MERINGUE SHELL

- 6 egg whites (from large eggs) at room temperature
- 1 1/2 cups of super-fine sugar
- 1 pinch salt or cream of tartar
- butter
- flour

CHOCOLATE SAUCE

- 3/4 pound semi-sweet, dark chocolate, cut in small pieces
- 1/4 cup of water
- 1 stick sweet butter
- 1 dash Kaluha or rum (optional)
- 1 dash milk (optional)

Put the chocolate and water in a bowl and melt over a double boiler. Blend in the butter and beat with a whisk. Add the rum or Kaluha or milk—or all three, if you want.

Beat the egg whites and the salt (or cream of tartar) until peak stage and then slowly add sugar and continue beating until the egg whites are very stiff.

Butter a baking sheet and dust with flour, shaking off all excess flour.

Fill a pastry bag with meringue mixture and pipe out a 3-inch diameter circle, working inward in a spiral to fill in the circle with meringue.

Cook in a 150°F. oven for 3 to 4 hours, until the meringue is hard. (That seems like a low temperature, but if the oven is too hot, the meringue will turn brown before it's fully cooked.) Turn off the oven, but leave the shells there until they've cooled to room temperature.

Cool and store in an airtight metal container. They'll actually keep for weeks.

ASSEMBLY

Sandwich ice cream between 2 meringue shells. Coat the sides with whipped cream and roll in sliced, toasted almonds. Drizzle hot chocolate sauce over this tasty dish and serve.

Serves 6

Profiterole au Chocolat

4 eggs (at room temperature), beaten
1/2 cup butter, cut into small pieces
1/8 teaspoon salt
1/8 teaspoon sugar
1 cup water or milk
1 cup plus 2 tablespoons flour

In a heavy saucepan place water or milk, butter, salt and sugar. Cook over low heat. When butter has melted, bring to a boil and add all the flour at once, stirring quickly with a wooden spoon. Beat vigorously until mixture forms a ball and leaves the sides of pan clean. Remove pan from heat. Let cool for a few minutes. Without returning pan to the heat, add 1 egg at a time, beating vigorously after each addition, until thoroughly mixed. You've got the right consistency when a small quantity of dough peaks when dropped from the end of a spoon. Use the dough immediately.

Preheat the oven to 425°F.

Place mixture in a piping bag and pipe it onto a lightly buttered cookie sheet in small 1 to 1 1/2-inch mounds. Reduce oven to 400°F. and bake mounds for 10 minutes. Then reduce to 350°F. and bake about 25 minutes more. Don't take them from the oven until firm to the touch. Cool away from any draft.

When cool, cut in half and fill with coffee ice cream. Put halves back together and put in the freezer.

Put a small amount of sweetened whipped cream in the center of a plate. Place 3 profiteroles in a triangle on top of the whipped cream. Drizzle hot chocolate sauce (see page 102) over each of the profiteroles and then put a little whipped cream between each.

Serves 6

Cold Soufflé Grand Marnier

1 quart of whipping cream
12 egg yolks
1 pound granulated sugar
1/2 cup Grand Marnier

Whip the cream until it's stiff. Beat 12 egg yolks, 8 ounces of sugar, and 1/2 cup Grand Marnier in a separate bowl until fluffy. Then add the whipping cream and whisk lightly. Beat the egg whites and remaining sugar until it's stiff. Add the egg-white mixture and fold together lightly.

To prepare the soufflé dish: wrap with aluminum foil or waxed paper collar around the rim of the dish about 2 inches high. Divide the filling among the dishes. Set to freeze for at least 4 hours. When ready to serve, remove collar, and pour raspberry sauce over it.

Serves 6 to 8

Cheesecake

"Qu'ils mangent de la brioche." (Let them eat cake.)

—MARIE ANTOINETTE

(MAYBE SHE MEANT CHEESECAKE, MAYBE SHE DIDN'T.)

This is the most dangerous recipe in the book. Not because of the ingredients, but because of the proportions. It's the way they prepare it at Fandango—5 cheesecakes at a time.

It's delicious, but it's too much for home consumption. You can freeze it, but if you're really hungry for cheesecake, it takes too long to thaw it out.

When I get the craving for cheesecake, I head for my favorite restaurant. Hey, it's only a ten-minute ride from my home to Fandango. Believe me, for cheesecake this good, it's worth it. Enjoy!

- 10 pounds cream cheese
- 3 pounds granulated sugar
- 6 envelopes of gelatin
- 20 eggs and 8 yolks mixed together
- 2 lemons (squeezed)
- 2 caps vanilla
- 1 1/4 pints heavy cream
- 3 pounds Graham cracker crumbs
- 4 1/2 sticks of butter, melted
- 5 buttered 9" springform pans
- sour cream, vanilla, sugar topping

Mix 1 pound of sugar with the gelatin and stir well. Mix the Graham cracker crumbs with the melted butter until they get mealy, then shake them into the buttered pans, pressing them onto the bottom in a layer about 1/4" deep.

Beat the cream cheese (at room temperature) in a large mixer at low speed.

Add the lemon juice and beat some more.

Add 2 pounds of sugar, the vanilla, and the cream. Then add half of the egg mixture.

By now the mixture will be building up on the sides of the mixing bowl. Stop and scrape the buildup back into the center of the bowl.

Add the rest of the egg mixture. Stop and scrape.

Add 1/2 of the gelatin and sugar mixture. Stop and scrape.

Add the rest of the gelatin and sugar mixture. Continue to mix until it's all blended. Stop the mixer and start spooning the mixture gently into the pans.

BAKING

Oven should be preheated to 300°F. Place a cup of water at the back of the top rack and place 2 cakes on a cookie sheet in front of it. Do the same on the middle rack. Then place 1 cake on a cookie sheet on the bottom rack with a cup of water in front of it.

Bake for 45 minutes, then reduce heat to 275°F. and bake an additional 15 minutes.

Cool cakes, then chill them in the refrigerator.

Serves 40

"Right time, right place, right companions."

—Sufi Saying

Acknowledgments

First I want to thank my two partners in this project, Jeff Whitmore and Mort Levitt. The three of us were guided by a simple philosophy: "Maybe we can accomplish something, if we don't take ourselves too seriously."

I'm especially thankful to Jeff for his research, interviewing, and overall collection of data. Beyond that, I appreciate the writing and editing skills that he brought to this book.

Mort is in many ways the father—or at least Godfather—of this project. Without his energy, intelligence, and ability to bring talented people together, *Fandango*—the book—would still be as elusive a fantasy as Fandango—the restaurant—once was.

I also want to thank Melissa Thoeny, our designer. Besides being a talented professional with a terrific eye, she's bright, cheerful, and incredibly patient.

Much thanks is also due Patrick Tregenza, whose vivid photography captures not only the day-to-day reality of Fandango, but its very spirit.

I'd like to give special thanks to Julie Levitt for her role in food styling, as well as for her editorial assistance.

And then there's the cast of thousands—or at least it seems that many.

These are the people who offered us variously their time, talent, and insight. Without them there wouldn't be any *Fandango*—the book.

They are: Pierre Ajoux, Marietta Bain, Pierre Bain, Peter Borowiak, Will Bullas, Paige Burks, Wesley Cain, Frank Charland, Basil (Bill) Coleman, Pedro De La Cruz, René Cruz, Les (The Barber) Fulgham, Walter Georis, Anne Germain, R.J. Gruber, Pat Hathaway, Hank Ketcham, Helaine Koffler, Elena Lagorio, Elmer Lagorio, Penny Lopez, Lynn Lumbard, Ray March, Denise Marseguerra, Susan Mehra, Tom O'Neal, Elena Rhodes, Guillermo Rios, Susan Schelling, Kathy Scherzer, Chris Shugart, Rita Shugart, Susan Shugart, Kathleen Spahn, Julie Still, La Tania, Will Wallace, Jim Webb, and Claire West.

I'm also grateful for the kindness of the people at the Pebble Beach Company, at the AT&T Pebble Beach National Pro-Am, and at the Bancroft Library.

I owe a great deal to the dedicated staff at Fandango. They are a professional and hard-working group of people who keep the wheels turning.

Finally—and especially—I want to thank our wonderful customers who come to Fandango to enjoy the "Cuisine of the Sun"—and a little bit more. Without them there'd be neither *Fandango* the book nor Fandango the restaurant.

Let the dance begin.

"Panso pleno joio meno."
"A full belly brings joy."

—Provençal Proverb